i

THE
PAJAMA EFFECT

BOBBE BAGGIO, PH.D

THE

Pajama

Effect

SUCCESS SKILLS FOR WORKING AND LEADING IN A VIRTUAL ENVIRONMENT

BOBBE BAGGIO, PH.D

ADVANTAGE LEARNING PRESS

NEW YORK. BOSTON. LOS ANGELES

Advantage Learning Press is a division of Advantage Learning Technologies, Inc. The logo is the trademark of Advantage Learning Technologies, Inc. All rights reserved.

First Edition: January 2014

ISBN: 978-0-9914051-0-7

LCCN:

For K1, K2 and K3

TABLE OF

CONTENTS

FAST FORWARD

This book began as Chapter 8 in a textbook that I wrote with Dr. Yoany Beldarrain, in 2011. That book, *Anonymity in Digitally Mediated Communications: Trust and Authenticity in Cyber Education*, was the first and last textbook I will ever write. I knew when I wrote the chapter I would write the book. I have been dealing with the virtual workplace for almost 15 years now. I have seen many really good, reliable, smart and creative people struggle. I became very interested in what behaviors people needed to succeed. In early 2011, I began conducting research. I surveyed many virtual workers from all over the country. I had conversations and held focus groups. *The Pajama Effect* is a result of that research. I thank all the ASTD (American Society for Training and Development) chapters that participated, all the volunteers who took the survey, and all the people who agreed to have the critical conversations and share their thoughts and frustrations with me.

I also want to thank everyone from the DLA (Distance Learning Association) annual events put on by the University of West Georgia and ASTD, as well as the many corporate, organizational and non-profit virtual volunteers who agreed to pilot test the RAI, or Respond-Ability Index. Your input and comments helped me make the RAI easy to use, online and readily available to everyone.

The purpose of the RAI and this entire project was, and is, to help people. Always remember that the respond-abilities are behaviors and behaviors can be changed. You can learn any of these with enough desire and practice. Also keep in mind that the secret to changing behavior is changing thinking first.

The 21st century will continue to bring us an avalanche of expansive change. Some of the technologies that I used as examples just a few years ago when I started this project are now obsolete. As we move forward in the 21st century and become more entrenched and dependent on virtual workers, we will find it necessary to teach these skills at a younger and younger age. Everyone can benefit from the ability to respond and not react, but for people in the virtual environment, this ability is essential.

Finally, I would like to thank my family. My husband, Alex Baggio, and adult children, Bert, Alexa and Tori, have been listening to me talk about *The Pajama Effect* for quite some time now. I thank them for their patience, thoughts, encouragement and input. And I thank them for their friends, some of whom made the "Meet…" sections in Chapters 4 – 8. I also thank my learners, colleagues and friends who gave me support and encouragement.

I am sure *The Pajama Effect* will be with us for a long time to come. Our ability to adapt to change and new environments, even though we are out of our element, is what makes us human and what makes our evolution so exciting and blessed. The rate of change with technologies has not, and will not, slowdown in the foreseeable future. As we move forward, it will be even more important to be in charge of our own responses. After all, we can't control people, technologies or the future; we can only control ourselves and how we respond to those continuing forces.

INTRODUCTION

Increasingly available new technologies and ways to connect have caused radical changes in the ways humans communicate, blurring the lines between different aspects of life. *The Pajama Effect* is the result of these changes. It describes a psychological and behavioral shift human beings experience when working in a physically detached and virtually connected world. This change puts them out of their element and vulnerable to a new environment, isolation and other challenges.

The economics of the 21st century has inspired companies and organizations to embrace the virtual environment to both increase productivity and lower costs. Digital technologies have given us increased speed, connectivity and independence. These advances offer us a more flexible and mobile way to work and live, yet the impact of these technologies on human beings is only beginning to be understood. The digital age came upon all of us with excessive speed. The rate of change and adaption is unlike anything we have ever seen, and that rate of change is increasing.

The online world has little respect for time, space and place. The 9-to-5 day no longer applies in a 24/7/365 world. It is difficult to know when work stops and play starts, or when to call it a day and say, "Enough is enough." People work from home, cars, hotels, and just about anywhere in increasing numbers. Telecommuters and workshifters have grown in number to more than 50 million workers and that is probably an underestimation. This also impacts learning, schools and training. Almost no industry is impervious. Even if you are a landscape contractor, with teams of people digging in the dirt, chances are you connect remotely and use technologies to accomplish some of what you do. The tools that connect us, and how we use them, are limited only by our imaginations. This ability to connect from anywhere with anyone is now part of our social fabric. We are all becoming a part of a technologically connected global culture that blends work, play and learning online. This affects every facet of our lives.

We are more connected and we are more mobile. We have access around the clock to colleagues, friends, family and shopping. All of this connecting has increased distractions. People are texting when driving, in meetings and in the checkout line. We need many conversations about what is appropriate and when, yet those discussions seem to be missing from our daily lives. The same scenes play out in restaurants, meeting rooms and homes: instead of focusing on being out to dinner with our significant other, we are on a cellphone, responding to a client; instead of listening during a meeting, we are texting our kids; instead of relaxing on the sofa, we are checking work emails.

The impact of this connectivity and our response to it has affected the way we live and our language. From LOL (laughing out loud) to TTYS (talk to you soon), we have created shortcuts that are acceptable in the digitally connected world, shortcuts that are more informal and increasingly more accepted. Just a few years ago, the digital world was seen as less-than, in education, publishing and many other areas. All that has changed. Newspapers are struggling to keep print versions alive; more students than ever are taking online courses, with 18 of the top 20 universities offering MOOCs (massive online open courses) for free. Language is what connects us and describes the way we live our lives and view ourselves. Our world is becoming more equal, more democratized and more open. The structures, boundaries and limits of the 20th century are breaking down both in society at large and in our personal lives. We can work with people around the globe and never leave our own home. Remaining connected and working or playing from anywhere is simple enough, thanks to technology.

This constant connectivity has influenced the way we act and react to its intrusion. Expectations are changed as roles and boundaries are blurred. Our personal time is vanishing and our schedules are becoming more flexible. We blend different roles, multiple tasks and new ways of doing things. There is an impact on human identity – on who we are and how we behave. Working, playing and learning have become so blended in our society that being ubiquitous has become second nature. We expect instant access and, for the most part, we get it. Instant access has become a necessity for getting things done and for our way of life.

Thanks to these technologies, the norms governing how we interact with coworkers, friends, family and society are also changing. *The Pajama Effect* has altered the expectations and approaches that came with us from the industrial age. There are conscious and unconscious elements at play in the virtual world. It is quite possible for virtual workers to be more productive, more relaxed and more in control of their lives but it is also possible for the exact opposite to occur.

It all depends on how each individual thinks and behaves – on the ability to respond and not just react. Distractions abound in the virtual environment, from advertisements, websites, social media and video everywhere to family obligations and love. The virtual environment can pull you off task and out of your element. To be successful working and leading in this new environment, you need to possess certain abilities.

The Pajama Effect has an impact not only on you, but it will influence the culture for generations to come. The future will be filled with remarkable challenges. We are in a unique position, leading the way forward on the technological frontier. It is our responsibility to teach the new generation skills it will need to be successful in the future. Although the challenges faced will be much different, the underlying struggle will be the same: the next generation will have to respond to changes when the boundaries and constraints of today's workplace have been removed. There will still be only 24 hours in a day, and 7 days in a week, and 365 days in a year.

The good news is those challenges can be met not just by where we work, but how we work. The virtual workplace has characteristics very different than most traditional office environments. The digital office is characterized by openness, vulnerability, personal privacy, informality and detachment. As a result, we have increased flexibility, less external direction and a different kind of stress. There are things we can do to balance personal and professional responsibilities. This balance is essential for success.

New technologies will continue to unfold. Holograms, artificial intelligence, virtual reality and faster, more integrated gadgets are sure to play a role in future forms of communication. These, too, will cause us to re-evaluate our psychological states and behaviors. *The Pajama Effect* will continue to be part of how we blend our private and professional lives for a long time to come. We will always have to find new ways of coping with unavoidable changes. The environments that we consider normal now will soon be outdated and replaced. Once again, we will be out of our element and dealing with a new environment where the boundaries and constraints no longer apply.

1

Why Go to the Office?

"Work spotlights the character of people: some turn up their sleeves, some turn up their noses, and some don't turn up at all."

-- Sam Ewing

Over the course of a year, 50 million people worldwide will begin the day by waking up in the morning, pouring a cup of enthusiasm and then walking into their offices in pajamas or whatever suits them.

Whether that "office" is the kitchen table, the basement or a hotel room, these individuals experience unique benefits – but not without challenges. Take Kelly, for example, who enjoys the flexibility of working from home because she has a small child. Yet, on any given day, you may find Kelly simultaneously doing the laundry, chasing her 3-year-old and typing a report, all while she waits for a scheduled web conference to begin. Then there is Robert, who used to get up at 4 a.m. to beat traffic and make it to the office on time. His new job is remote but requires that he collaborate with his teammates on a regular basis. His teammates, however, don't live on the same continent; one is in Madrid and the other one in Beijing. Both Kelly and Robert cannot successfully perform their jobs unless they make mental and physical shifts.

The term "workshifting" is used to describe what happens when people find themselves working out of trains, hotel lobbies or from their kitchen tables (Lister & Harnish, 2010). The idea of working or going to school in your pajamas is not a new concept. There are plenty of ads out there highlighting the advantages of working or learning through digitally mediated tools. Among the advantages portrayed: staying in your pajamas or, at least, not having to wear business attire. Currently, there is increased interest in working virtually because organizations now rely on technology to do more with less.

The Pajama Effect, however, is more than changing your work location from the traditional office space to a corner of your home or hotel room. *The Pajama Effect* is a state of being where you find yourself out of your element and where normal constraints and boundaries no longer apply. *The Pajama Effect* involves a psychological and then behavioral shift. To function best in this dramatically different environment, you must focus on what it takes to be successful in the virtual world. This new workplace wilderness is an environment that is physically detached, where the conventional structure of the workplace has

9

vanished. Interruptions and distractions abound, making it difficult to get the job done.

The Pajama Effect is a phenomenon brought about by the breaking down of walls. This absence of tradition and structure creates flexibility and new responsibilities affecting every facet of personal and professional life. Smartphones and digital communications have changed the 9-to-5 workday to a 24/7/365 never-ending cycle. You find yourself answering work emails while watching your child's baseball game or texting your friend during an Internet-based business conference. There are more demands placed on your time than ever before and instant responses are expected. *The Pajama Effect* helps you understand what it takes to function successfully as you work in this detached yet highly connected and demanding world.

EMERGENCE OF THE VIRTUAL OFFICE

How did we get here? It all happened very fast, and there are no signs of it slowing down. For example, the story you may read today goes viral within 24 hours but then, within another 24 hours or less, it is considered old news. New fortunes are made and reputations are destroyed overnight. There is no time for psychological gestation or conscious absorption before we are on to the next thing. The pace at which we live is continually becoming faster.

It is important to understand how we got here in order to see where we are headed. Let's take a trip down memory lane, back to the year 1999. That certainly was a big year; it may have been the year of biggest change. Situated at the dawn of the 21st century, in 1999, we were surrounded by exciting technological advancements yet many of us went to the office wearing a suit and faithfully following a 9-to-5 routine. We did not realize the potential of these advancements. In the meantime, programmers around the globe scrambled to make sure 1999 could turn into the year 2000 and the earth would keep on spinning. (Remember the fears about Y2K?) Even after all the 9s safely became 0s, some of us were partying like it was 1999 because we did not fully understand how technology was affecting our lives. Radical and dramatic changes had already begun.

The year 2000 doesn't seem that long ago. Mark Zuckerberg, founder of Facebook, was in high school. Google was an infant corporation and Microsoft was the evil empire. There was no iPad, no iPod and no iTunes. We had Learning Management Systems, but Web 2.0 was only a buzzword and the presidential election depended on counting votes on punch-style paper ballots. As we moved to a 3G network, connectivity increased, as did outsourcing and the use of digitally mediated communications. The barriers of time and place were slowly but permanently being blurred, affecting individuals, organizations and society at large.

The impact of these technological advancements is evident in the swift economic changes that now affect how you earn a living, especially as the economic position of the United States on the world stage has changed drastically. With the dollar value plummeting, only 36 percent of the top 500 global companies are now U.S.-based. China, the sleeping giant, has awakened and taken the lead in many areas of commerce. Brazil, Russia, India and China (known as the BRIC countries) are some of the fastest growing economies in the world. These, by the way, are the same countries to which the U.S. outsourced manufacturing, technology, accounting and production jobs not so long ago. The outsourcing trend altered western economies, making them no longer based on the production of goods or services. As a result, these economies evolved to include the "knowledge worker" (Lesonsky, 2011) as a key player in a company's success.

The term "knowledge worker" originally meant one who works primarily with information or who develops or uses knowledge in the workplace. In today's workplace, it commonly describes individuals who are experts in a certain subject area.

For a brief moment in time, it seemed that knowledge workers were not part of the outsourcing trend. Then technology caused the world to shrink, opening previously unforeseen possibilities. Knowledge workers in remote locations emerged. The lines between knowledge and information blurred, but both became available without anyone having to leave home.

Today, information and expertise are shared in nanoseconds, regardless of geographic locations or time zones. Whether it is the outsourced doctor in a remote country who reviews your child's x-ray while you wait at your local emergency room, or the programmers in India who write the code that runs the New York Stock

Exchange, knowledge is shared around the globe. Many positions are staffed from the global labor market and many jobs today require virtual teaming and collaboration. This new type of worker is not bound by traditional office rules. Today's worker has the challenge of adapting to the demands of the virtual office. Digital connectivity has made knowledge a temporary thing, because new knowledge is generated constantly. Even new products and ideas are quickly outdated because someone else across the globe builds and creates a new product or idea. As Bill Gates reportedly once put it, "Intellectual property has the shelf life of a banana."

The changes affecting our global workforce are broader in scope than just the change from factory worker to knowledge worker. Because we have gone from stationary to mobile and from analog to digital, the make-up of the global workforce has rapidly changed. Many baby boomers and digital immigrants now find themselves out of jobs, struggling to go back into a job market dominated by technology. Digital immigrants by definition are all the folks who were born before the PC age, even if they owned the original Atari or played Pac-Man or Pong. Unless they update their skills, these digital immigrants stand no chance when competing in the job market with digital natives, who were born surrounded by electronic technology. Digital natives work online, they live online and they socialize online. They expect technologies to be part of how they live, work and play. They do not know life without digital connectivity.

Even though the majority of workers today still work in a traditional office, more people find themselves workshifting. In 1995, when author and computer expert Woody Leonhard wrote, "Work is something you do, not something you travel to," he probably realized that what affects the bottom line of a business is that the job gets done, regardless of location. The terms "telecommuting" and "telecommute" were first used by University of Southern California researcher Jack Nilles in 1973. Today, telecommuters may work from home a few hours per week or the entire week. If you are one of them, you may or may not work in your pajamas and you may or may not have to collaborate with someone in a different time zone, but the effect is the same. You are working remotely and you live by connecting in the virtual environment.

In this book, the terms "virtual worker' and "pajama worker" are used interchangeably to mean a person who uses technologies to work, play or learn virtually. The terms "virtual office" and "virtual workplace" are used interchangeably to describe where the virtual worker "works."

The virtual environment is very different from that of a traditional office. You are not in a physical location provided for and directly controlled by your employer. As a virtual worker, you work from home, on the train, at coffee shops, airports and soccer games. You use text, chat, conference calls and virtual meeting applications. Your daily commute to a physical location is replaced by technologies. All of these changes affect the way you work, play and learn.

"Virtual" means that people are functioning in cyberspace in one way or another. You live, work and play in a world connected by digital communications that does not require you to meet face to face in order to conduct business or maintain social relationships. In the virtual environment, you are detached physically but connected by technologies. Society at large has been transformed by the new methods of communication. Now there are critical behavioral components necessary for success in this digitally connected environment.

The emergence of the virtual office is an inevitable byproduct of these technologies. Some see the emergence of the virtual office as annoying, scary or even as an unacceptable way of doing business. Others embrace it as a "growing pain" that companies must experience in order to survive tough economic times and forge new markets in a global economy. Bottom line: Organizations that do not embrace the change will sooner or later be swept under by it.

Because the global economic infrastructure is so interconnected, dramatic changes in the way we work have spread rapidly regardless of the industry. Businesses that fail to adapt to the changes brought about by technology will find themselves unable to compete in the global marketplace, making their products and services either outdated or obsolete altogether. The traditional office is no longer able to support the needs of postindustrial economies, and it certainly cannot sustain the development of innovative new business models.

Before the digital age, the business landscape included defined roles, time boundaries and explicit face-to-face communication. Companies found it challenging to find qualified employees from a limited geographical pool of applicants. The emphasis was more on a firm handshake than on the ability to build trust through a well-written email. Today, however, the employee enjoys more flexibility but also more responsibility. The workday is fluid yet it merges with personal time, often blurring the lines between both. Communication today is woven and integrated into every aspect of the workday. This communication is more abstract, contextual, text-based, qualitative and emotional than ever before. Companies expect their employees to be able to seal the deal, no handshake needed; an email or a recorded video conversation will do.

What does the new workplace look like? It looks like wherever you are – your dinner table, home office or hotel room. Its quality is influenced by the technology you use, the social conditions you are in and the productivity stress you are under. It takes the form of the nature of the work you do, and the pressures and the challenges you face. It takes on the inexorable traits of human nature. You may be working on the road, in your basement, in an automobile or on a plane; you may have a 24/7/365 workweek. This new workplace is without the limits and boundaries you took for granted in the old office. It is ubiquitous. It is everywhere, ever-present and always turned on. It makes demands on you that the human psyche was not made for.

Characteristics of the Virtual Office

The virtual workplace has distinctive traits that are very different than most traditional office environments. The virtual office is characterized by openness, vulnerability, personal privacy, informality and detachment. It must be open, flexible and grounded on a common business vision.

This means that the virtual office is never really closed, yet its hours of operation are flexible. We check our email on the go via our favorite gadget and we can reply from the gym or the dentist's office. To be open also means that we must be open to new ideas and new ways of doing things. We cannot rely on old habits or old configurations. Success depends on relationships grounded in a common business vision and working together toward a common goal. Just as in the traditional office, only more so, if a team member does not believe in the overall mission, the rest of the team will feel the burden and have to pick up the slack. The virtual office gives you more and easier places to hide, escape and make excuses. Lack of contribution will eventually diminish trust as well as the power of collaboration.

Management of virtual workers requires expectations that are clearly stated and adhered to. As you may already know, organizational culture depends on the perceptions of its members. If the stakeholders distrust leadership, the organizational culture will suffer. The organizational leadership is ultimately responsible for uniting the virtual workers under a common vision. Sometimes this can be very difficult, especially if the virtual worker is more open and flexible than the leaders. There needs to be a balance between openness, flexibility and the cohesiveness of the team. You may be able to march to the beat of your own drum, but eventually you must also be able to join the band.

In the virtual workplace, you are very vulnerable to change. You must expect the unexpected. Change is the only constant. You will be in a state of perpetual motion unless you learn how to stop and breathe. There will always be something new to learn, whether it is how to use a new technology tool, develop a new strategy or acquire a new skill. Change also comes from your ever-evolving priorities. Very often you will find yourself moving, changing or shifting – not only office locations, but work and life priorities, responsibilities and connections.

The flexibility inherent in the virtual office provides you with more personal choices. If something goes wrong, you simply change your approach. Sometimes you will have time to reflect on the situation, but other times you will be hard-pressed to trust your gut and make an instant decision. The pajama worker has more personal privacy than the person working in the traditional office. Some of the expressions of this privacy may be obvious, such as working in your PJs because you haven't gotten dressed yet or in your bikini so you can work on your tan. Other reasons are less explicit, like finally being able to go with your child on a school field trip, or hiding from the world – unshaven and wearing the same shirt – until the project is finished. The point is, when you shift from a traditional office to a virtual one, you will feel a new sense of personal privacy within your physical world.

The demand for aligning your connections will force you to come out of your cave and join the other virtual inhabitants. You will be expected to collaborate across boundaries of time, space and disciplines. You will be expected to contribute your expertise but also synthesize and evaluate the contributions of others and make decisions that are best for the task you have been entrusted to complete. You will often feel like a fish out of water, trying to understand the perspectives of those from other cultural backgrounds. You are also likely to be placed in a team of individuals you have never met before, and have no idea if they can be trusted.

The virtual office is highly informal but results-oriented. There is no dress code and no official lunch break. You must determine what works for you and how you will handle interruptions. Who will get the door if you are on the phone with a client? How will your spouse notify you if the toilet leaks? Who will take care of the barking dog during your web conference? These are all informal but important protocols. They are rules you must establish in your household, because no one wants to hear your barking pooch when they are trying to participate in a webinar. Such interruptions also give the impression that you are unprofessional and informality should not be confused with unprofessionalism. Everyone loves babies, but when they are crying in the background it is impossible to get the job done. The virtual office is not a way to hide out and escape the business world.

Informality should have no direct impact on the end results. In the virtual office, you want to focus on the goal and use project management techniques to track your own progress. You want to learn to measure how your energies are spent and where the time is going. The responsibility to get the job done rests with you and no one else. As a pajama worker, you are responsible for seeking help when needed and tapping into the right resources to maximize your productivity. This is definitely a results-oriented environment (Gregory, 2010).

Finally, the virtual office is geographically detached but you are always able to be connected. You may have to get up earlier than expected or stay up five extra hours in order to speak to a virtual colleague or client who is in a different time zone. Your device may beep while you are in the shower and instead of reaching for the towel, you reach for the phone. Low and behold, it's the purchase order you were hoping for. All is well. This scene is not too different from what is now known as the "smartphone prayer." The phrase is used to describe the physical stance people take when secretly working on their smartphones during face-to-face meetings, in airports or restaurants, on dates, at the ball game, and pretty much everywhere they feel the urge to "check in": they carefully hold the phone with both hands, head bowed, quietly but intently typing on the screen. There is always more room for improvement, however, as someone posted on a blog, "The smartphone prayer is a plea to God to abolish the damn things."

In the virtual workplace, you want to be able to respond to the pressures of this new way of life. Such pressures are constant and they come from all angles. The verb "respond" evokes counter action of some sort, which is exactly what is needed in this environment to not only get the job done, but also to stay afloat in a sea of professional and personal demands. The technology beckons you to stay connected; it "trains" you to provide and to expect feedback. As a result, you create new habits, some good and some detrimental to your success. Each message you receive reinforces your response to "check in."

Our ability to respond to this stress can and will make or break your success on the digital frontier. Just like the explorers and industrialists needed skills that matched their time in history, the virtual worker needs certain abilities to thrive. There are five essential *respond-abilities* needed to thrive in the digital jungle: 1) act with autonomy, 2) set and enact priorities, 3) be authentically productive, 4) make responsible choices, and 5) align connections. Later in the book, we will explore these respond-abilities in more detail and learn how as individuals we can develop responses that are advantageous.

The emergence of the virtual office has pushed dramatic changes upon us all. For right now, let's reflect on the following point: It is the characteristics of the virtual office – openness, vulnerability, personal privacy, informality and detachment – that compel us to learn new behaviors in order to cope with challenges and flourish in this environment. It is essential that you learn how these characteristics affect you, personally and professionally. You also want to understand what the consequences of all these changes may be. Only then will you be able to acclimate yourself to the new environment and achieve success.

The pace at which we communicate has increased and so has the physical distance. Yet the technology tools we use to communicate make the increased physical distance a non-issue. You are expected to do more in less time, process more information faster and remain connected with practically no "off" time. Pajama workers behave in different ways and react differently because they are under different workplace stressors. In the virtual work environment, the practice of deliberately responding and not reacting is paramount.

WHY WOULD YOU WANT TO WORK VIRTUALLY?

You may choose to become a virtual worker or your company may simply send you home to work. Either way, you should be aware of some of the pros and cons for both you and your employer. After all, there are two sides to every coin. Advantages of the virtual workplace definitely outweigh the disadvantages for your employer, and it can be the same for you. First, working in the virtual office saves relocation time and travel costs, for both you and your employer. Second, productivity tends to be greater and development times shorter. Finally, it is obviously a convenient commute.

The new workplace is more responsive to connection and likely to increase a company's knowledge base because remote employees must share their knowledge with team members to get the job done. This new environment values creativity, self-assessment, reflection, and high performance standards. The pajama worker must be able to problem-solve and make critical decisions. Companies can also access the best resources, including talent, at the cheapest prices, keeping costs down. Individuals working remotely often feel a greater degree of freedom, personal privacy and autonomy. Leadership can organize teams along functional lines or cross-functional lines according to need, without being concerned about each individual's physical location. Organizations have an unprecedented level of flexibility, cohesiveness and connection. Both product development and commercialization can be achieved from the virtual office.

There are also a few disadvantages to the new workplace. Interaction must be intentional rather than accidental because there is a lack of physical contact. You will no longer run into the boss or a colleague in the break room; you will no longer be able to walk by your colleague's desk and discuss the next project. Things by necessity are done in a more intentional and structured way but may not require the same level of formality, which may sound like an oxymoron. The virtual workplace defies traditional power structures and minimizes formal protocols. For example, if you have a question, you have to seek out someone who has the knowledge you need. This can be achieved via a phone call, an instant message or a text message. The entire Internet is your knowledge base and you don't have to wait for the next meeting to get the information you need. You generally do not wait to speak to your supervisor unless it is absolutely necessary.

Responsibility is evident in the procedures you follow when working remotely because the virtual worker is held accountable in different ways than the traditional worker. While this is not necessarily a disadvantage, you may struggle with a new way of "keeping track" of the work you do. In a traditional office, "working" is often defined by the worker being physically present. The assumption is made that if you show up to work then you are working that day. This is far from the truth.

In the virtual office, "working" is defined by getting the job done. If the job does not get done, then the virtual worker did not "work" in the eyes of the boss. This brings about the need for more structure with clearly defined expectations. Technology tracks your positions and progress, when you are logged in, how long you were logged in, your email chat history and the web pages you visited. Some companies even install invisible programs on company-issued laptops so managers can spy on their remote employees. Managing the pajama worker is certainly a huge concern for employees as well as employers.

Before you shake your head in total abhorrence of these stealth technologies, you need to understand that the managerial challenges of the virtual workforce are exponential. These challenges are complex and related to distance, culture (internal and external), language and time, to name only a few. Cultural and functional differences may lead to a variety of different thought processes and obstacles. The freedom and mobility you experience can negatively impact productivity if you are left without support. All virtual workers need support and training on an ongoing basis as well as encouragement from leadership.

The virtual employee must feel trusted not only by his peers, but also by the boss. In his book, *The Speed of Trust*, Stephen R. Covey points out that trust equals confidence; therefore, when a supervisor trusts his employees, he is confident in their abilities and their integrity. In the virtual office, trust is at the heart of everything. Employees must be treated like the professionals they are and allowed to do the job they were hired to do. Mistrust has the tendency to rear its ugly head when management does not understand the needs of the virtual worker, or when the virtual worker does not understand the expectations of management. Trust issues in the virtual environment are imminent.

Noted management scholar Peter Drucker was one of the first to talk about management by results. In 1959, he coined the term "the knowledge worker" and indicated that management of knowledge workers was going to be one of the challenges for the 21st century. Although Drucker lived to see the beginning of the virtual workplace, he died at age 95 in 2005, the year Facebook was being launched (Drucker, 2006, 1964). It was Drucker who first brought us the concept that employees were valuable and should be considered assets of the company. Drucker said that what was important to the company was achieving results; management by observation was from an era that has long since disappeared. More credible than ever, his theory of management by results resonates in the virtual workplace.

Measuring productivity is more difficult when you can't do it by observation, so it presents another challenge in the virtual workplace. In the industrial age, productivity was highly tied to specialization. Performance was much more measurable when it was immediately observable, or so we pretended. In the virtual workplace, both performance and productivity must be evaluated differently. The degree to which a person is productive has to do with more than just what he/she does and where he/she does it. It is inexorably tied to the systems, procedures and people interacting with the virtual worker. In order for the virtual worker to function, the organization must define and communicate organizational goals, objectives, vision and mission. It must train virtual workers but also train managers to provide expectations, directives and evaluate the success of the project not only at the individual level but also at the team level.

Technology has made it possible for communication to become more multi-dimensional. Rather than only providing closeness or connectivity, you can manipulate digitally mediated communications to transmit or seek information. Today's social media revolution has also caused countless office quarrels and caused some individuals to lose their jobs because of something they posted on a social networking site. Take Michelle, for example, who faithfully updated her Facebook profile every morning. One day she commented on how stressful her job was and she was immediately terminated for negatively influencing co-workers. Then there is Octavia Nasr, who was fired from her position as Middle East editor for CNN after she tweeted about her political sentiments, which were considered to be anti-American.

Remember: everything you say online can be used against you. Digital never forgets.

The idea of meaningfully connecting to others has really never changed. Today, however, we are inundated with so much information that the ability to meaningfully align communication with purpose is challenging. One common mistake is to blame technology for this dynamic shift, but it is the catalyst, not the cause.

Technology is a strong driving force behind change in human behavior. It provides different vehicles through which we communicate. You may choose to call from your smartphone, send an email or text. Each of these options is merely a different mode for delivering your message. It is humans that change their behavior when using technology, regardless of delivery mode. For example, think of the last time you went out to dinner with a friend or relative. And, instead of focusing on you, the other person became engrossed in a text exchange with someone else. Maybe it was the other way around, and you were the one paying more attention to your smartphone than to the human being physically next to you. Opportunities for communication abound but so do unintended consequences and the potential for chaos.

Humans by nature want to be effective contributors. The ways, means and methods of contribution in this digitally connected world are different. The rules are different. The playing field is different. We communicate differently and we interact differently. The patterns for sharing knowledge, learning and collaborating have also changed. Now you can record everything that is being said or done. There is a traceable record of everything in the virtual workplace. This alone certainly changes the way you learn, share and interact with others because you know you are being watched. While you may enjoy more personal privacy than the traditional worker because you can create your own work environment, as a virtual worker you actually have less professional privacy because the technology is constantly capturing your whereabouts. There is no turning back.

The world in which we live, work and play has changed. These changes are all-encompassing. They are omnipresent, universal and pervasive. In a 2007 report on unified communications, Frost and Sullivan Corporation characterized the growth of the virtual workplace as "one of the biggest business changes to hit in years." The human interactions that we have traditionally emphasized no longer suffice. The look in someone's eye may have to be determined online. We work, learn and play in a virtual world where we may never meet face to face with the folks we interact with. We work for companies we have never been to and we achieve degrees without setting foot in a classroom or on a campus. These new types of interactions have unforeseen consequences. This change in human interactions impacts individuals, organizations and society at large.

Today's virtual workplace is an environment full of stimuli. You are left to your own volition to turn off the cell phone, turn off the computer and disconnect from the demands of the virtual office. You are on your own to seek relaxation, joy and down time. The problem is, you do not know how to do this without feeling guilty. Only when you are able to act with autonomy, set and enact priorities, be authentically productive, make responsible choices, and align connections will you be able to get things under control and reap the benefits of the virtual workplace.

WHY SHOULD YOU CARE?

When Alexander Graham Bell shouted, "Mr. Watson – come here – I want to see you!" in 1876, he could not possibly have predicted that the basic idea behind the first telephone would morph into digital smartphones with so many capabilities. He probably never anticipated how his new gadget would forever change the way people communicate. The same idea lies behind current technologies. The technologies that connect us today will look completely different tomorrow. And they will inevitably impact the way you communicate when working, learning and socializing.

Even up to the present day, most people are still only talking about the technology itself and what you can do with it. The technology may be different, but the conversation is the same. *The Pajama Effect* forces you to reflect on your behaviors and ask yourself: "How have these behaviors changed because of how I use technology?" You live in this rapidly changing, digitally mediated world; consequently, there is no alternative but to care about what is happening around you. Even if you did your best to ignore it, you are immersed in it. Even if you are the last person on the planet to get connected, the fact is that your child, your spouse, your friend, your neighbor, your sibling or your co-worker is already connected, and the changes in his or her behavior will in turn have an impact on you.

No matter what you do for a living, your boss already expects that you have certain technology skills and that you can apply them in your day-to-day responsibilities. If your boss feels you would benefit from professional development, he or she may ask you to participate in an online training course or a hybrid course that has face-to-face components. The reality is that it is not cost-effective for companies to pay for your travels or for a day "off" for training purposes only. Many companies will now expect you to complete special training sessions online, but on your own time. When this happens, you cringe, bite your tongue, but eventually succumb to the pressures of the changing workplace. Let's face it: you want to keep your job. Without realizing it, you are blending your work life with your private life and learning through digitally mediated communications.

You should care about *The Pajama Effect* not only for your own sake, but also for the sake of the generation that follows. Whether it is your child, your niece, goddaughter or best friend's kid, younger people will face new challenges in the workplace of the future. You are positioned to be a pathfinder and role model for the next workforce. It is your responsibility to teach newer generations the skills they need to be successful in years to come. Although the challenges they will face will be different, the underlying struggle is the same: they will have to respond to changes around them as the boundaries and constraints of today's workplace have been removed.

The influence of technology on behavior is undeniable. You are part of an always-connected network of individuals, ideas, agendas and challenges. Your time is in high demand. Your boss may expect you to check your email on Sunday morning or your spouse may want you to answer text messages while you are writing a business proposal. You may have to stay home Saturday night and finish an assignment for an online class.

We react to these changes in many ways; sometimes successfully, but other times we stare into space, frustrated. We wish that someone could show us how to get everything done within the 24 hours a day we have been given.

The good news is that there is a way to work it out. It relates to not just where you work, but how you work. As you now already know, the virtual workplace has characteristics very different from most traditional office environments. The virtual office is characterized by openness, vulnerability, personal privacy, informality and detachment. As a result, you have increased flexibility, less external direction and you may experience a different kind of stress. There are things you can do to balance all your personal and professional responsibilities and diminish the stress you are under. This balance will let you be productive and successful.

Today, we have digital technologies; tomorrow, it may be something else. Holograms, artificial intelligence, virtual reality and faster, more integrated gadgets are sure to play a role in future forms of communication. These will cause us to modify and re-condition our current behaviors. This means that *The Pajama Effect* will continue to be a part of the way we blend our private and professional lives for a long time to come. We will always have to find new ways of coping with the unavoidable changes. The environments that we consider normal now will soon be outdated and replaced. Once again we will be out of our element and dealing with a new environment where the boundaries and constraints no longer apply.

As stated earlier, technologies have been a driving force in establishing *The Pajama Effect*. This new behavioral and physiological phenomenon affects the individual, the organization and society. It is highly unlikely that the changes that have already taken place will ever be reversed. You must be in a position to survive the sea of change but also to emerge as a valued professional and balanced individual. To be successful in the digital environment, you need to manage the skills you have while learning new skill sets, new perspectives and improving your ability to respond to the pressures around you.

When you hear yourself saying things like, "I am trying to make the best of the situation," ask yourself if this is becoming an excuse. Trying your best means giving yourself the opportunity to learn the skills you need to be successful and get the tools necessary to make it happen. Or, as Star Wars character Yoda famously said, "Do. Or do not. There is no try." The privacy you have in the comfort of your virtual office may cause you to do things you would not do in the traditional office space.

The digital world is one of dichotomy: on one hand, there is a sense of privacy, but on the other hand everything is being recorded by the communications. Be aware of the traps you set for yourself, the excuses and the negative self-talk: "I tried doing it and it didn't work out, so it's okay." Light your own path and arm yourself with the courage to say, "I will succeed," and believe it.

2

What Causes *The Pajama Effect*?

"The difficulty of writing about dramatic change in the midst of it occurring is that the very drama of the effects unleashed by the change will be mistaken for what the future will become"

-- Kent
Spreckelmeyer

The Pajama Effect is caused by the human condition: delicate, fallible and vulnerable to change. It influences workplace conditions as well as professional and personal expectations. It causes us to think differently and behave differently than we would in a face-to-face office. All of the wonderful technologies we use now are merely catalysts in the virtual environment for behavioral change and newfound freedom. This influences how we respond or react to others and to ourselves. The technologies themselves, although constantly changing and becoming more powerful, allow but do not control *The Pajama Effect*. The virtual environment provides us with opportunities for freedom, yet that freedom is never really free; it always has a price.

Telecommuting, workshifting, telemarketing, virtual conferencing and online learning are all just a part of the new social order. Connecting with digital devices has given rise to a new way of doing things, a way that requires humans to act in new and different ways. Some people are very successful and thrive in this new environment and some need to go to summer school. *The Pajama Effect* is more than just a frame of mind. The lines between work and home have been blurred. There are new standards for those working in the virtual environment. Based on a survey by Wakefield Research of 1,013 American virtual office workers describing what they do while officially working from home: 43 percent watch TV or a movie; 35 percent clean house or do chores; 28 percent cook dinner; 24 percent have a drink; and 20 percent play video games. It used to be easy to separate work and life. It was simple in a 9-to-5 world. You went to the office and that was work. When you came home, that was life. Clear, simple and easy. Not so anymore (Business Wire, 2012).

Jack Nilles says, "The whole point of teleworking, from the employee's point of view, is the ability to fit one's work into the rest of one's life, not the other way around, as is the case in the 'traditional' office. The point of teleworking, from the employer's point of view, is that its bottom-line benefits (productivity gains, space savings, employee retention, etc.) far exceed any feared risks of losses" (Wong, 2012).

After years of working, learning and teaching in this environment, I became interested in what made some people thrive and others falter. I learned through research, observation and interviews that success in the virtual environment has nothing to do with prior success in the face-to-face world (f2f), nor is it necessarily related to your age, occupation or education. My research revealed that there are critical behaviors that cause some individuals to adapt positively to this new environment. Those folks who adapted well to working and living in a virtual environment actually enjoyed what they were doing. They saw working virtually as an opportunity to experience freedom, independence and self-rule. They were able to act. They were able to accomplish things that supported their success.

These pajama workers were able to manage the innumerable interactions, situations and jumbled circumstances that intermittently interrupted their day. They were authentically productive. In fact, they were more productive than they had been in a more traditional environment and they knew it. A study supported by Stanford University found that, despite all the distractions, telecommuters were actually more productive than their peers in the office (Kossek & Hannum, 2011). Those who thrive in a virtual office swear they are never going back to the cubicle. They get more done and they have more fun.

The opportunities and unexpected consequences in this environment are always revealing themselves. "It's just too much" is a common reaction of new pajama workers to the virtual environment. New ways of communicating and organizing become evident. Your interactions and schedule are constantly being modified, and so is your self-identity. This new environment allows you to define a new identity and persona. Some of your prominent positive traits may surface or, perhaps, your salient negative traits get the best of you.

This environment allows you to observe others. Like Harry Potter and his Cloak of Invisibility, you can float through the digital landscape undetected. You may learn to examine the interactions of others without being recognized, but this sense of anonymity is often false and misleading. In reality, you may be silently followed, and your digital fingerprints and footprints tracked. So you experience both more freedom and a sense of privacy but at the same time a sense of uneasiness, vulnerability and being monitored (Stillman, 2011).

Regardless, many are able to juggle the high demands of the workplace and personal life with ease and confidence. So the question arises: How do you handle things in the virtual workplace? What do you do when you hear a message coming in? When your cell phone rings? When you have to choose between work and family? Most of us, most of the time, react. You shift consciousness and react to the device, the intrusion of a technology, a response to a stimulus. *The Pajama Effect* is all about acting and not reacting.

DRAMATIC CHANGE

It was not so long ago that the Internet did not exist. We had no digital connectivity. That is how it had always been. Then it all quickly changed and so did our options. The workplace became more open, flexible, freelance, collaborative and far less secure. It has dramatically changed and we are not going back to the good old days.

Technology has not only changed where you work, but, more importantly, it has changed how you work and what you work on. You work in a place interconnected and supported by digital connections. The demands of your work are very different than just a few years ago. Technology has irreversibly changed your life. Digital technologies have played a dynamic role in overcoming the constraints of the physical workplace. We are liberated to be more creative and enjoy more freedom. These new technical dimensions have become a dynamic and integral part of almost every organization. New behaviors have emerged as a result of technology, with radical changes in how we work, learn and play. *The Pajama Effect* cannot be avoided but you can adjust to it.

We mix traditional functions and new roles in this digital workplace. Technology enables us to change our private and professional boundaries. It is increasingly difficult to distinguish between work and play, between leisure time and office time, between private and public. This can wreak havoc in our lives. The same technologies that made connecting easier have made it more difficult. And there are the challenges of the technologies themselves, and how leadership supervises and deals with virtual employees. Defining who you are personally, as a team member and even organizationally, requires deliberately created formal and informal virtual support systems.

Today, 50 million U.S. workers, or 40 percent of the work force, perform duties that could easily be completed from a remote location (Telework Enhancement Act, 2010). Most people who workshift do it on a part-time basis, often due to issues of trust, but more organizations are acclimating to the virtual workplace. It is not just the corporate sector that has recognized telecommuting as a means to save money and increase productivity. The Telework Improvements Act of 2010 requires U.S. federal agencies to enact plans that will encourage employees to work from home. In 2008, 17.8 million people in the U.S. worked remotely at least part-time. In 2009, there were 102,000 federal government employees reportedly working from home. By 2013, the number of remote U.S. employees in the public sector is expected to increase by 65 percent, while the private sector is likely to increase the number of remote employees by 35 percent (Fortier, 2009).

After experiencing a slow adoption rate, European countries are also expected to increase the number of teleworkers, with the United Kingdom and Germany taking the lead. In a 2004 survey, 77 percent of British employees said they would work from home if given the option by their employer. As a result, in 2007, 46 percent of British companies offered the option of workshifting, a sharp increase from 11 percent just three years earlier (Lister & Harnish, 2010). The significant global increase in virtual

39

working will continue to cause rapid and radical changes to the individual, the organization and to society.

Even if you are not sure about workshifting, there are enticing monetary benefits to working from home at least part of the time. It is estimated that telecommuting could save you between $2,000 and $6,800 per year, because you will drive less and spend less money on work-related items. That translates into a savings of about $170 billion per year in the U.S. alone (Hill, 2011). Many politicians in favor of a green world also support telecommuting. As of this writing, several bills have been introduced or re-introduced in the U.S. that would benefit telecommuters. These include: the Parents' Tax Relief Act, promoting home-based work and telecommuting tax credit; the Telework Tax Incentive Act, to provide tax credit for purchasing equipment used for telecommuting; and the Telecommuter Tax Fairness Act, which would eliminate any state-based tax on interstate telecommuting.

Servers located who knows where connect us around the world. The global village, a term coined by Marshall McLuhan in the early 1960s, has now come to pass. The future is expected to look more like the Semantic Web, where machines are able to interpret the meaning behind information. Although the Semantic Web is still a dream, recent advancements such as cloud computing create new levels of connectivity that will continue to foster new social behaviors and workplace paradigms (McLuhan, 1964).

Permanent connectivity and ubiquitous communication has both advantages and disadvantages. The office moved from the cubicle to the cloud and, here we are, working in our pajamas. *The Pajama Effect* affects the individual, the organization and society. There are different levels of human interactions within the virtual environment. There is the individual worker or learner, the virtual team, the virtual organization and the virtual society. Success starts at the individual level and then moves toward the organization and/or society (Baggio & Beldarrain, 2011).

THE INDIVIDUAL

Technology has changed the very structure of who, how, where and what you do. In the virtual workplace, you have minimal physical contact with other human beings and rely heavily on verbal communication. As a virtual worker, you may interact with colleagues either synchronously in real time, or asynchronously in delayed time. Whichever, you are likely to be tethered to and dependent on a screen or a mobile device. Technology has freed you in some ways and enslaved you in others.

Today, many people work away from the main office or organization because they can stay connected in so many ways, whether they want to or not. We are all part of this huge shift. There is an ever-growing array of technologies, tools and options. These technologies have invaded our lives very quickly and not even researchers have had a real chance to study the long-term implications or influences. According to an NBC report, by the end of 2010, there were about 5 billion cell phone subscriptions worldwide (Pramis, 2013). Because of the allure of always being connected, many people cannot and do not disconnect. They are afraid they might miss something.

For the virtual worker, the isolation of working from home is a real issue. If you are working from home for the first time you may experience a type of culture shock. You may feel apprehensive and not contact colleagues for help, because you were used to walking over to someone's desk to ask a question. You may not intuitively know what to do after drinking your morning coffee. Developing specific strategies can minimize the feeling of isolation, but it does not happen overnight. All of a sudden, you may realize how many house chores you have pushed to the side and may even get the urge to do them when you should be working. You may become intensely aware of the schedules for everyone else – the kids, the dog, the mailman – but be unaware of your own. You may even experience loss of your sense of identity, especially when there is no need to wear a suit and there is no physical pat on the back.

You might be in trouble when you allow technology to take over your work life and your personal life. You can become hooked, fixated or addicted to being "connected" at all times. If managed effectively, the use of digitally mediated communications can free you to be more efficient and enhance the quality of your life. Dangers abound; embedded in the challenges of digital communications is the opportunity for miscommunication. The social conditions of the virtual world do not provide the opportunity to observe and monitor the other person's physical behavior. This lack of non-verbal cues forces you to infer the tone of written communication, or the tone of the other person's voice. The message is inevitably interpreted based on the receiver's own perceptions. For this reason, messages can easily be misconstrued.

The frequency and timeliness of communication becomes more important in the virtual office. This is because what is expected of you has also changed. Another potential pitfall is inappropriate feedback or the lack of any feedback. Providing open and honest feedback in a virtual environment is vital. You must learn to listen carefully to the other person, provide clear feedback, and also ask questions to avoid misreading or misinterpreting messages. You are expected to provide a speedy response to emails and phone calls because everyone knows you are connected through the technology. This, too, adds to potential stress. You are feeling enslaved because you're always "on." You are stuck and you do not know how to get unstuck.

It is much easier to focus on work at the office because it is a defined place with a defined appearance. There are cubicles, desks, colleagues and the supervisor's office. In the case of a brick-and-mortar school, there are fellow students, the teacher and the white board. In cyberspace, none of these traditional visual clues are available to you. The new virtual office is comprised of a combination of text, audio and very different visuals than the traditional workplace or classroom.

Collaboration skills are in demand and somehow you are expected to know how to work collaboratively. You are also expected to use collaboration tools, run a web conference or work in a virtual team. These are not skills that come naturally to most of us, and they were most likely not taught in school. They are not even taught by most training experts. If you already have these skills, consider yourself lucky.

These changes have affected the structure of your family as well as your workplace. There is a much higher demand for flexibility in terms of role and function. Listening skills have morphed into being able to listen with your eyes and not just your ears. Instead of work becoming easier, it has become more demanding, more time-consuming and less predictable. Psychological and physiological stressors have increased.

The traditional work environment provides certain familiarity and structure that makes many employees feel safe. When you work virtually, you are responsible for creating your own safe environment. With remote work, you do not get what many employees expect to receive when working from the office cubicle where the furnishings, space and equipment all provide an environment that supports you. Technology advancements have already caused changes in the organization's infrastructure, products, services, leadership philosophy and, yes, its employees. With technology, nothing ever remains the same; change is the only true constant.

THE ORGANIZATION

At the organizational level, *The Pajama Effect* impacts the role of leadership. It changes the priorities when evaluating or managing workplace performance. Organizational expectations have changed, placing added value on knowledge and skills instead of seniority or title. The workplace has become one of outsourcing and the outsourced. The virtual workforce is geographically and culturally dispersed. We are here, there and everywhere. Because the virtual worker must be able to act with autonomy, organizations are becoming flatter. There is a palpable struggle between the traditional need to control employees and the new flexibility virtual workers must have in order to get the job done.

Connectivity allows companies to successfully outsource work around the globe. This is a huge paradigm shift in the business model, not only for manufacturing but also for the business process in general and the workplace. Teams consisting of internal, external, first-, second- and third-world labor replace the old face-to-face models, forcing businesses to re-evaluate their processes and reinvent themselves. Even small Mom-and-Pop businesses can have a supply chain that reaches around the globe. The entire business environment is rapidly evolving into a more complex and highly interactive space. Interactions facilitated by social software and real-time audio and video tools are supporting collaboration and driving product innovation.

Since its infancy, communications has been an integral part of an organization's business structure. In the old workplace, informal communications used to take place at the water cooler, in the lunchroom or at the bar after work. External communications were always a little more removed except for golf outings, sales expos or dinner meetings. These external communications were always designated to a few particular folks while internal communications were carried out according to the organization's hierarchy and structure, organizational culture or its policies.

Today more than ever, the state of an organization depends on the organization's leadership, decision-making process and quality of communications, most of which are conducted via technologies. Our behavior has changed so much that even if we are all sitting around a conference table, chances are that we received the agenda via email prior to coming to the meeting. What used to be communications through very clear channels and organizational structure is now less predictable, clear and stable (Sarkiunaite, 2008).

There is always something new to learn; you will never know everything you need to know. Management has the challenge of training those folks who are already part of the organization plus the challenge of training newcomers. Not everyone can do it and not every organization is ready for what is transpiring. One of the characteristics of success for *The Pajama Effect* is openness and the ability to align connections. In an interview, the director of the MIT Center for Digital Business indicated that openness is an important cultural trait for any business in the digital workplace (Meyer & Meyer, 2002).

Because the organization itself is getting flatter, few middle managers have survived in the new workplace. So now there is more to do and fewer people to do it, yet companies have no intention of hiring or resurrecting that management hierarchy ever again. You are forced to be more autonomous, often realizing that only you are responsible for your job and career. Many organizations believe it has become more effective to hire just-in-time consultants instead of full-time workers. Micro-workers, consultants, experts and telecommuters are the workforce for the 21st century. The dynamics of this can be detrimental unless leadership understands how the consultants will be able to fit in and work remotely to accomplish the given task.

The collaborative abilities of virtual workers are paramount in the new distributed environment, but collaboration in most cases is not a strength of group members. The presence and awareness that was available to you in a physical environment vanishes in the virtual world. This is usually replaced with some version of the groupware or social networking tools currently available. The actual environment where work takes place is left up to you as the pajama worker, your home life or your default location.

As of 2008, an estimated 8.4 million workers were members of virtual teams. Not only will these numbers continue to escalate, but so will the challenges. The stress and problems these individuals face are often underestimated, as are the setbacks for leadership and the organization as a whole. These challenges include communicating and coordinating efforts across time and space, interpersonal relationships, knowledge and trust. Working toward a common goal is more complicated when you work with colleagues from different backgrounds, viewpoints and cultures. This is already difficult when you live in the same country, let alone when you live on separate continents (Borowicz, 2007).

Financially speaking, organizations are reaping the benefits of sending employees to the home office. A 2010 report by Lister and Harnish states that organizations that allow employees to workshift are likely to save well over $10,000 per employee, even if they worked half-time from home. When you can work where you want, where it is convenient and where the company does not have to pay for office space, your company is quick to add up the savings. It also allows more mobility for the company to hire people from labor markets where the rates are less expensive. The report shows that this could easily translate to saving $400 billion a year in the U.S. alone. Should we expect companies to ignore this money-saving proposition? Absolutely not. Indeed, experts estimate that by 2019, industrialized nations will see an explosion of telecommuters, with 30 percent of employees workshifting at least two to three days per week (Baker, 2011).

Such radical shifts create a sense of insecurity and fear of the unknown because no one can truly predict all the ramifications. The changes experienced by the individual and the organization are extended to the society at large. The impact of teleworking is far-reaching. There are many good reasons for recent dramatic changes in the workplace: less hierarchy, more flexibility and a focus on results. The new environment will change because of more virtual workers, exactly how it does, no one can be sure.

THE SOCIETY

Although it is not clear what the workplace of the future will look like, it is safe to make certain assumptions. For example, the behavioral changes experienced by the individual will become accepted norms within larger groups, eventually influencing society. Things are terribly intertwined in cyberspace. Many behaviors and actions are related to social and technological dimensions, giving way not only to new behaviors but also language. Sayings like: "Hey I Facebooked you!" or "Tweet me" treat these sites as if they were action verbs.

Social networking has redefined the way you maintain contact with relatives, friends and co-workers. You may intuitively post a short message on someone's page instead of calling. Maybe you zealously guard your private life and never accept requests from colleagues. Whatever your inclinations, you are probably communicating very differently than you did just five years ago. You are not the only one.

This is also true of business practices. We certainly do not conduct business today the same way we did five years ago. There is a new understanding of what it means to be global, multicultural or international. Years ago, the word "international" likely meant that the company had offices overseas, or had overseas clients. Today, "international" has been replaced by the word "global," which encompasses more than just geographical locations. It includes values, ethics and morality of culturally diverse individuals. Many values and business practices considered to be more Western have made their way around the globe. The main language of the Internet was, and is, American English.

A good example is the traditional business letter, which has morphed from a formal ink-and-paper document to a more open, friendly email. Then, after a few email exchanges, many businesspeople start addressing their new contacts by their first names. Some countries where business was traditionally conducted in formal ways may resent this Western influence, yet it is part of the new way of forming relationships and building trust. It's a behavioral change that begins with the individual and permeates the organization, then society and eventually becomes an accepted norm.

Behaviors that blur the lines between private and professional are not always positive, yet this change is a global phenomenon. The real problem is that this blending is not always done in a way that acknowledges the value of either part of your life. Often it is your private life that is ignored and your family starts to resent your virtual job. Globally, this is taking a toll on the family, quality of life and on the planet's stress level.

The costs and benefits of working in the virtual environment affect society locally as well as globally. There are benefits from saving money, having convenience and not commuting. Energy savings impact everyone involved: communities, employees and employers. The virtual workplace:

- Reduces traffic congestion, accidents and greenhouse gases
- Saves fuel, reduces energy costs, global warming and terrorist targets
- Reduces the threat of pandemics, health risks, reduces medical costs and increases productivity
- Improves work-life balance
- Reduces the carbon footprint, saves oil and energy
- Saves companies an average of $20,000 per employee annually
- Frees up 15 to 25 workdays a year in commuting time
- Saves 9.7 billion gallons of gas -- $38.2 billion a year or $138.80 a month per worker
- Diminishes Persian Gulf imports by 37 percent
- Makes people happier; 79 percent of workers say they would like to telecommute
- Prevents over 95,000 accident-related deaths and injuries (Telework Coalition, 2011)

These are just some of the benefits to the economy and the global community's well-being. As more individuals and organizations embrace working virtually, even more benefits are likely to emerge. Yet there is always the possibility that the increase in virtual work will also create more challenges. The more we all learn about how to respond in the virtual environment, the better prepared we will be to face these new challenges.

3

How Does The Pajama Effect Influence You?

"Between stimulus and response there is a space. In that space is our power to choose our response. In our response lies our growth and our freedom."
                                        -- Viktor Frankl

How different is the workplace of the 21st century? Our old systems of social interactions – the schools, the businesses and the relationships of the past – are vanishing. The old systems focused on compliance. In a world of innovation and connection, compliance just doesn't cut the mustard. Compliance and autonomy are on two opposite ends of the stick. The virtual frontier requires self-reliance: no excuses, no victims and no alibis. The endless blending of work and play, family and profession forces you to think independently. It forces you to re-examine your priorities and get out of your silos. The virtual world is always on. There is no more waiting for the bell to ring so you know it is quitting time. Because you are always connected, you see the world as an interconnected, interdependent place.

The virtual workplace is more flexible, friendly and open, but also more removed. This causes us to react to each other differently. We change the way we establish and communicate our goals, desires, outcomes and intentions. In this new world, things have to have a purpose; your time and alignment are valuable. Things need to flow and flow with relative ease. There is a requirement for meaning that integrates one aspect of your life with another. There is less room for arbitrary acceptance and more desire to make everything count.

Information is everywhere, available to everyone and available instantly. It is only a click or a swipe or a voice command away. Text messaging is replacing the phone call. Quick little bites of thought are rapidly expressed and easily tagged. Information without purpose is useless. Every gadget, computer, TV or device is flooding you with an abundance of useful and useless knowledge. Too much is available and too little can be retained. You can find infinite amounts of information in any format – audio, text or video – or any combination. The "because I say so and I am important" law of value is dying. The professor or politician is no longer the authority. Old rules about what is important to know, and why, no longer apply. We are crowdsourcing, social networking and collectively collaborating.

The old paradigm of competition is being replaced by a new one of collaboration. Nothing is off limits or out of bounds. You cannot collaborate if you are not capable of acting independently. Stephen Covey points out in the *The 7 Habits of Highly Effective People*: first you have dependence, then independence, and then interdependence (Covey, 1989). Our society cannot have interdependence with dependent people. We are coming out of an era that fostered dependence. The industrial culture, unlike the agrarian culture before it, did not teach and/or support acting with autonomy.

During the age of agriculture, the world was independent out of necessity. Industrialization brought economies of scale and dependence like the world had never seen. Dependence on oil, dependence on government and dependence on substances: This is how we live. We are dependent on our cars for our very lives. We drive everywhere: to the store, work, and soccer game. The world became more closed during the era of industrialization. It was us against them. We had industrial espionage and highly protected national and trade secrets. That worldview has changed. We are now looking at an open-source standard.

Crowdsourcing has replaced the view from the C-Suite. Closed minds, closed doors and closed connections are no longer valued. Top-down has turned bottom-up. Grassroots are in, boardrooms are out. Open-source and sharing epitomize the way of the 21st century. What just a generation ago would have been labeled "cheating" is now embraced as open collaboration among learners or workers.

Closed is the way of the past; the 21st century requires an open-door policy. Being open to everything leaves you open to being vulnerable. You get messages that summon a response while you are at home on a Sunday night, but it is 8 a.m. in India and you are not sure the message sender is a credible source. This is a big change in how we communicate and it affects us on all levels.

There is nothing new about change. As humans, we have been changing forever. It is what we do and we call it life, evolution, the great progression or unfolding. When there is change, there is always some confusion. Physicists tell us that nothing changes without going through an altered state first. Teachers will tell us that if we are not a little confused, a little anxious and a little challenged, we probably aren't learning anything new. So the idea of change, confusion and evolution is not new. What is new is the speed of change and its continued acceleration rate.

Our digital connectivity has accelerated the speed and rate of change. We talk about "speed of connectivity" and mean 3G, 4G, 5G and someday maybe 25G? Who knows what the future holds? In 2002, our world was 3G and we made the move to 4G in 2011. The speed at which we connect and exchange information has increased by 25 percent in barely a decade.

The speed of information and news, both good and bad, traveling around the globe is faster. Things can go viral much faster now. The speed of trust has increased and so has the speed of distrust. Time has accelerated because we no longer take time off. A 24/7 clock runs online all the time, continuously. It is all happening now and it is NOW...somewhere and everywhere.

This openness has led to a polarity about whom and what we are: we are both more isolated and more connected. We have more privacy but far less privacy in a way the world has never seen. Not only can the digital "Big Brother" track a conversation you had on Facebook, it can tell the last website you searched on Google and where you ate last night at 6:15 p.m.

Although we are more detached, we are also more defenseless in many ways. Polarity rules our world. We take things for granted. We trust in the banks, the automatic doors and the pipeline valves that open and shut automatically. We trust when we pull up to the pump that the gas will be there. And when we sign on to the Internet, we expect to connect and make it to our destination. We trust that the GPS is telling us the truth. We can work in our pajamas. We can be everywhere but nowhere. We are more connected but less associated. All of this polarity is leaving us quite psychologically unprotected.

Expediency and expectancy have changed the way we live. Adjusting to change is something we just do. There is nowhere to hide but we feel like we are invisible. We send text messages so that we can say what we want to say when we want to say it. We'd rather write remotely than speak directly. It gives us the freedom to express ourselves and the cover to de-individuate – to leave behind the persona we have created in favor of expressing freely who and what we want and who and what we are. With this freedom comes the ability to push boundaries, to recreate and redefine our limits. We can explore new frontiers and become new individuals.

Carl Jung used the term *individuation* to describe this: "In general, it is the process by which individual beings are formed and differentiated; in particular, it is the development of the psychological individual as a being distinct from the general, collective psychology" (Jung, 1971). Our definition of self is changing rapidly. We are no longer dependent on the three dimensions of circumstances, people and events. These no longer define who we are. Connections do. Our connections are changing the way we view ourselves and others.

Average isn't average because we have the ability to compare everything to everything else. All you have to do is search for it...and there it is. The visibility, reach and expansion of our knowledge are at an all-time high. OK is not OK any more. It was OK when that was all we knew. We didn't know any better. In this world driven by speed, data and examples from all over the globe, we know what good is, we are pretty sure we know what right is, and we sure know what connected is. We have universal access to everything. And with this we have begun to develop a universal consciousness. We are holding each other to higher standards but we are holding ourselves to higher standards, too.

Technologies have given us the ability to carry out our ideas. We can make our thoughts a reality. Publishing and presenting our ideas is easy. The world is flat. The world now belongs to the doers, the practitioners. It is no longer enough to figure out what has to be done. The time has come to take responsibility and do it. The layers of hierarchy are being eroded. You get to respond directly to every ringtone, every email blip and every chat ping.

Respond-ability…is your aptitude for leading your destiny in the virtual world. Responding is acting and not reacting.

The virtual world is an environment that is much more flexible but much less secure (Altman, 2009). This is a place without the typical walls or boundaries established in the physical world. It is also a place where mental and emotional walls can tumble down. Digital technologies have given us the ability to connect but remain isolated by letting us work in our own space, mostly unobserved, and in charge of our own destiny.

To lead in this highly connected, interdependent world, you want to respond to it in a self-determined, independent way. You want a personal skill set that allows you to function at a very high level. You need the freedom and autonomy to develop new and authentic solutions to very real problems. You need to stay connected in a way that is beneficial and allows you to get the job done.

THE FIVE ESSENTIAL RESPOND-ABILITIES

Our ability to function in this new workplace environment is highly dependent on our ability to function as happy, healthy, well-balanced people. The five respond-abilities of *The Pajama Effect* are learned skills. All of us want to know how to survive and thrive on the digital frontier.

Some of us do this well and some of us may need a little work.

The five "Respond-abilities" in *The Pajama Effect* are:

1. Act with autonomy
2. Set and enact priorities
3. Be authentically productive
4. Make responsible choices
5. Align connections

ACT WITH AUTONOMY

Autonomy is the capacity of the individual to make independent, un-coerced and rational decisions. To act with autonomy, one must first think with autonomy. This sounds like an easy task but in a world bent on controlling your thoughts, influencing your purchasing power and presenting your nightly newscasts based on ratings, it is not as easy as it sounds. Autonomy suggests the ability to listen to an inner voice and be guided by morals and values that are beyond the basic standard. It is a self-governing principle that can lead you to beneficence and, ultimately, to your own happiness, success and fulfillment.

To act with autonomy, an individual has to act – and not react – to circumstances, events and individuals. It is a self-reliant ability that permits you to act with security on your own perceptions and to trust your own impressions of right and wrong. Self-reliance requires trusting and believing in your own ideas and abilities. It is no longer enough to be proactive or to feel empowered. In the virtual environment, you need to act in order to make things happen. You need to take control and keep control of your thoughts, actions and emotions. You need to recognize your special gifts, your talents and your shortcomings, accept yourself where you are, for what you are, and be OK with all of it. Because in the pajama workplace, you are almost always connected virtually when you are actually alone.

The distractions and protections of the cubicle are gone, so the excuses and alibis that once worked no longer matter. You need to be brave and put your heart into what you want to achieve. But before you can be brave, you have to be consciously aware of what it is you are thinking and doing. It is just too easy to mute the sound or walk away from the computer to do something else. There is so much to react to in the virtual environment: your family, your friends, your parents, the technologies, the lack of concentration, the vulnerability of too many moving parts. There are intrinsic and extrinsic distractions to react to and many things that can overwhelm you and pull you off course.

In *The Pajama Effect*, you are all alone much of the time. Autonomy requires you to be rational and aware. You want to focus on your heart and your motives, as well as the motives of all those around you. You need to see clearly, keeping your desires and intentions at the forefront. Be flexible, yet focused. You must believe and know that you are in charge of yourself. So you walk the walk and make the effort, with no excuses and no regrets. You are true to yourself. You need to give up life as a victim and take charge of what you create. Acting with autonomy requires you to take charge of your destiny.

If you live with guilt, resentment and fear, it is very difficult to act with autonomy. If others control you, by circumstances or by your environment, it is very difficult to act with autonomy. When you act with autonomy, you cannot go around judging everything everyone else does. In the virtual world, there are too many cues missing to do that and it is too easy to misinterpret things. There are emoticons and now videos but you still do not have the three dimensions. Autonomy is inner direction and inner knowing. You need to keep the focus on you.

You know when you are telling the truth and when you are not. You know when the computer really malfunctioned and when it didn't. You also know when you were really too busy because of work, or kids or parents and when that was just a convenient excuse. You know when what you are saying is, "I don't really want to do this now." In the virtual environment, you feel invisible and you are sure no one will know. But you will know. Acting with independence is not reacting with avoidance, excuses or alibis.

SET AND ENACT PRIORITIES

How you choose to spend your time reflects what's truly important to you. Time never stands still and neither does the virtual world. Lack of time is one of the most overwhelming aspects of modern culture. It causes stress, anxiety and fear. We take classes and read books on getting things done and on managing time. Time is a moving target. It just keeps going. If you are going to enjoy working in your pajamas, you must learn to set and enact your own priorities.

Time management is an oxymoron. You cannot manage time. You can only manage yourself. Time just is. There are 24 hours in a day, whether you are in Australia or New York, whether it is Sunday or Monday. There are only so many hours in a day, days in a month, and months in a year. It is impossible to manage time. Beyond the switch from daylight saving time to standard time or crossing the international dateline, beyond the meridians and the rules we have established for what time it is where, you cannot manage time.

However, you can manage yourself. You can manage your thoughts first and then your actions. Before you can enact priorities, you have to be able to set priorities and stick with them. They are your priorities: you can adjust them. You can determine what makes you feel overwhelmed. You can decide how to spend your time. Often, our perception of what is overwhelming is not real, it is just our perception.

Your attention is what you focus on and your activities are what you do. The expectation of being able to do it all simultaneously is one of the biggest stumbling blocks to success in the virtual world. New online teachers often feel overwhelmed yet, not to minimize the time it takes to successfully teach online, it is not a 24/7 job. But if you are thinking about anything 24/7, worrying about it 24/7 and agonizing over it 24/7, it certainly can feel overwhelming.

Worry, anxiety and fear will make anything overwhelming (Chidambaram, & Zigurs, 2001).

Because the virtual world never stops, it is critical to remember that you must stop. You are setting priorities and acting on them. Apply personal project management: set your priorities, determine your critical path, do the best you can and let it go. Release it and move on. You have done the best you can do, that is all you can do, so feel good about it. You determine what you want to achieve, put your attention on your priority and do what you can do to get it done. Then you move on to the next priority. When you are finished, you are finished. When you feel like you must always do more, connect more, interact more, your priorities will start to slip away.

Your own insecurities make you more vulnerable in the virtual world. Insecurity makes it difficult to enact priorities. You need to trust yourself and your ability to be dependable. To enact priorities, you need to know what you are doing is good enough and proceed without personal judgment, criticism, disapproval or negative commentary. You can neither manipulate or be manipulated or it will be nearly impossible to act on your priorities. You have to trust your intentions and everybody else's. If you have a bad feeling about something, ask yourself: "Why do I have this feeling? Is it based on fact? Does it matter to anyone? Does it matter to me?"

Virtual smiles are never very comforting or approving. If you are constantly looking for approval, you are going to have a difficult time with *The Pajama Effect*. By trying to be popular, conciliatory or compelled to connect, you can waste a lot of time. There are too many people, connected in far too many ways, to please them all. If you are comfortable, know what you want to accomplish and set out to get it done, you probably will. Trying to please everyone in the virtual world is a losing proposition. The digital world is always moving. Approval seeking might have worked with observation-run management or classrooms but not in the virtual workplace.

There are far too many choices to set and enact your priorities based on approval. Many virtual workers are afraid to turn off their devices for dinner because they think their clients or bosses expect them to always be available. Is that reasonable? Is it real? It is easy to read your perception of reality into virtual reality. Remember that personal perceptions are subjective anyway. So stay on the positive and confident side of life. As philosopher Ralph Waldo Emerson said, "Nothing is at last sacred but the integrity of your own mind."

You get to choose what you think. No one else can do it. Freedom starts from the inside. Psychiatrist Victor Frankl stated, "A human being is a deciding being." In order to set and enact priorities, you must learn to decide for yourself.

Extremely intelligent adults will make excuses, whine, fuss and just plain refuse to set and enact priorities because they do not feel comfortable. They do not want to feel vulnerable. In *The Pajama Effect*, you are vulnerable…you're in your pajamas, for heaven's sake…the next step is naked. You're vulnerable to the new, to the changing, to the different, to being alone, to being remote, to being vulnerable. One of the first steps to getting comfortable working in your pajamas is to get comfortable with yourself. You cannot set and enact priorities if you are not willing to take responsibility.

BE AUTHENTICALLY PRODUCTIVE

To be authentically productive, you must get past the idea of doing things in a prescribed way. One of the greatest things about the pajama workplace is that it gives you the freedom to create. You can create your own environment. To some extent, you can create your hours. You can even create the dress code. You have flexibility and you have choice. You have the freedom to work in your pajamas. We are wired to do things the way we have always done them. We are comfortable with what we know and very uncomfortable with what we don't know. I have seen very intelligent engineers, scientists and university faculty balk at the idea of communicating with new technologies. Nothing makes the individual feel more vulnerable than a new technology.

You have freedom so long as you get the job done. All this freedom will also let you procrastinate. If you want the freedom, you need to be able to trust yourself; then other people will rely on you, too. The proof is in the doing. The buck stops with you. You know when you are achieving what you want to achieve and you also know when you are not achieving. You have the freedom to create the life you want in the virtual environment. That is one of the reasons most people want to escape the constraints of the cubicle in the first place.

The virtual workplace is results-oriented and demands authentic productivity. There is a great deal of discussion these days about authentic thinking and learning. But the real question is…authentic to whom? *Authentic* means authentic to you. You must get past the idea of an objective right reality and move on to your best subjective effort. Being authentically productive requires using your creativity and applying your talents (Psychology Today, 2013).

There is no age limit to *The Pajama Effect*. This is not generational. In order to qualify, you must be continually willing to learn. Creativity requires that you stay "open at the top." You want to step out of the box you know as you and into the box called the unknown. You are carving out a path in a new frontier, setting the rules and creating the regulations in a new work environment. As your understanding of the rules of living in the virtual world evolves, so must your continual curiosity to know more. You can never stop learning in the virtual workplace.

Creativity requires freedom and freedom requires security. It is very difficult to be creative when you are fixated on being right. You can't think out-of-the-box when you are scared of being wrong. It will not work. The flexibility of *The Pajama Effect* has to leave you room to fail every now and then. When you are out of your element and dealing with change, you need a certain degree of creativity to produce. Creativity requires you to be comfortable with the unfamiliar. Creativity doesn't just happen; it takes energy, time, intention and focus. It takes the willingness to step into the unknown and do it over and over and over. This can be quite a task.

Although the virtual workplace is in some ways more comfortable than the traditional workplace, in other ways it is not. There is a sense of comfort in knowing where the edges are, where the limits and walls are. To learn more, we must be willing to step beyond those limits. This is not an easy or comfortable assignment for many people. It requires trusting ourselves to be able to progress and succeed. It also requires stepping into the unknown, again and again. Creativity requires us to let curiosity and inquisitiveness take us to unknown territory. Without both of these, we cannot learn; without learning, we cannot remain continuously curious.

Curiosity is the spark that ignites the fire, the desire to learn something new. It invites us to go beyond our boundaries and enter into something we have never done, thought of or examined before. We are born being curious about life but it is something that most of us do not manage to retain. Our education system and cubicle workplace certainly did not encourage or reward creativity. The 21st-century workplace is quintessentially encouraging to curiosity. This is an age where everything is changing at an alarming speed. Something is always new and must be learned. Change is the name of the game and it is everywhere. To keep up with change, you have to be inquisitive.

Inquisitiveness is the process of going one step beyond curiosity and finding something out. Ask the questions, clarify, process and then ask again and again.

Inquisitiveness is the rocket fuel of learning and what allows you to produce. It is what authentic productivity is all about: the ability to ask the question, then go find the answer, ask more questions and repeat. It is the commitment to find out and do what lets you use your talents and intelligence.

You are much more likely to be inquisitive about something that interests you. Interest and focus are strengths in the virtual world. Ideas come in all varieties – crazy, perfect, good and ridiculous. Interest and focus will help you determine which of these ideas is important to you.

With *The Pajama Effect*, in order to be authentically productive, you need to harness intrinsic inspiration. Focus on your possibilities and not the limitations. When you are attracted to an idea, pursue it without negative self-talk and internal negation or fear. All of the negatives will trip you up. Saying to yourself, "I can't, I don't have time, I am afraid I will mess it up, I have never been good at that, I am not really motivated, I know I should but…" will kill curiosity, kill creativity and kill inquisitiveness. When you are not intrinsically motivated to be productive, you won't be. You can only kid yourself for so long and eventually you will have to admit when you are being authentically productive and when you are not. How will you know? You are not enacting your priorities and reaching your goals. Things are not getting done.

One of the biggest limitations to the virtual environment is distraction. There are a whole lot of reasons why we are distracted but really it comes down to only one: because we allow ourselves to be. Distraction is what happens when you take your focused attention off of what you wanted to concentrate on and allow yourself to focus on something else. There are many kinds of distractions. Some are big and some small, some subtle and some abrupt, but all distractions are something that we allow to happen.

Reaching goals is a bit elusive for most people. This elusiveness is compounded in the virtual world. Procrastination will strike if you are not conscious of staying on task. There are more things to distract you, which is why it is even more critical that you master the art of focusing your attention. The key to being productive in the virtual world is pure and simple – focused attention. The concentration of energy and attention toward meeting a goal or achieving it will help you avert procrastination. Just the awareness that you are putting off tasks knowingly and not reaching your goals can help you avoid the procrastination demon. Procrastination affects at least 20 percent of people (You Are Not So Smart, 2010). That percentage may be much higher in the virtual workplace.

If you have a to-do list that goes on for pages and pages, it is going to be hard for you to feel a sense of accomplishment. It is also going to be hard for you to know when to "turn it off" for a while. This will lead to procrastination. If you can't get it all done anyway, what is the use? If you have too much to do, more than is humanly possible, why bother to do anything? Find a distraction and don't think about it for a while. Everyone procrastinates sometimes; in the virtual world, distractions are increasingly available. Procrastination in large part reflects our inability to cope with perceived pressures. Endless to-do lists give you another reason to put things off.

Authentic productivity is not arbitrary surfing, it is not net-wandering or aimless searching, it is not chatting or texting, it is not even responding to endless email. It is energy that is focused and concentrated on enacting your priorities. It takes clarity, concentration and directed energy to have focus.

Focus doesn't allow for excuses, doesn't act like a defeatist and doesn't get lost along the way. When you stumble or fall, when an obstacle gets in your way, when your Internet connection dies or the computer crashes, or whatever your latest challenge may be, if you are going to be productive in the virtual world, you must get up, brush yourself off, get back on target and focus. It is that simple – no, really – it is that simple. Distractions may happen but productivity and success require focus. The virtual world is more relaxed but requires a high degree of focus to be authentically productive.

MAKE RESPONSIBLE CHOICES

The buck stops with you. The digital workplace gives you many more options and holds you much more accountable for your choices. One of the biggest challenges people have is being able to be in control of their choices. Every response is a choice. You always have the choice to respond or react. As long as you are conscious of what you are thinking and doing, you have a choice. It is in your control, your power and your account. That means you can't blame it on someone or something else. The quickest way to let go of blame and victimhood is by becoming good at setting personal boundaries.

Boundaries come in many forms. There are physical, emotional, intellectual, time, effort and privacy boundaries. There are social, relationship, connectivity and response boundaries. There are many more. All of these boundaries are being blurred and changed by the new virtual environment. In order to act and not react to circumstances, events and people, you want to develop the ability to set personal boundaries, or limits. This becomes extremely important in the virtual world, which is seemingly limitless. Setting your own boundaries will help you to be less vulnerable and make responsible choices.

Vulnerability in *The Pajama Effect* happens on many fronts. You are more vulnerable because you are less guarded in a new element. You are not surrounded by the walls of expectation, nuances of structure and symbols of obligatory behavior you had in the traditional workplace. You are more exposed and more open to everything. Along with exposure comes sensitivity, and with sensitivity comes vulnerability.

Mixing business with pleasure requires you to make moment-to-moment choices and then align those choices with your priorities. There is no question that you are more sensitive to attack than you were within the walls of the corporate fortress. In the cubicle castles you had firewalls, security cameras, protocol and limits. In most cases, these reduced vulnerability. The Internet is a scary place; you are vulnerable to Trojans, worms, malware, spyware and viruses. But the virtual worker is really vulnerable to much more than that. The real vulnerability in *The Pajama Effect* comes from you being alone with you.

Success depends on the individual's adaptive capacity. Change in the virtual world is an everyday occurrence. The technologies change, the meeting times change, the kids' schedules change, and the virtual environment moves on. New innovations lead to change. Change can be rather unnerving. The ability to embrace change and welcome it into our lives is something we are all going to have to achieve. Overcoming fear is the biggest obstacle to embracing change.

Making responsible choices doesn't mean that you can't have fun in this new world. In fact, if you don't find a way to play and laugh you are probably not going to like it very much. One of the most important and responsible choices you will have to make is taking time off to relax. Get away from the emails, the chats and the connections. Yes, that is right; get out of the virtual world. Go for a walk, swim, play tennis, go to a concert. The saying used to be "unplug" but today everything is wireless, so just turn it off. You can do it although it is not easy. Like Pavlov's dogs, you have been conditioned to check emails, texts and messages, but it is possible to shut them off.

If you don't take time away to have fun and play, you are going to have a difficult time with focus. Without focus it is very difficult to make responsible choices. Some people can relax online playing games or talking to friends, but that is rare. Online is still on. You need to find the off button. The best way to do that is to get away and have fun.

ALIGN CONNECTIONS

You need to learn to be selective about your connections. The newfound freedom of 24/7 connectivity gives you the ability to connect instantly. There is also a need to connect well. In the virtual environment, both context and content have to be aligned a little differently. You can read a great deal about the amount of time people waste online, creeping around vicariously observing. Some research indicates the Internet can be highly addictive. Other research says that technologies cause us to become lost in cyberspace (Cash, Rae, Steel & Winkler, 2012). If you search the term "Internet addiction," you will find tests to determine if you are physiologically addicted to Internet browsing.

In the 1970s, parents used to say, "Teenagers today spend so much time on the phone." Psychological distractions abound over the years: the telephone, movies, TV or the Internet. There are also sports, newspapers, radios and substances such as drugs and alcohol – if you're inclined toward psychological escape you can find it with or without the Internet. These allow you to release your state of consciousness and drift off into another world.

What makes the virtual environment interesting and also what helps you to be creative is the ability to step beyond your definition of you. Carl Jung said we individuate; the

Internet allows you to de-individuate, or have the ability to step beyond your previously defined perspective of who you are. Digital communication brings with it anonymity, which allows you to de-individuate. This gives you more freedom, more responsibility and less accountability. It is an environment that brings out the best and the worst in people. If you're interested in cheating on your partner or pretending to be someone else, it is easier to do online. Want to waste time chatting when you should be working online, who will ever know? It is no accident that when you live online, you blend intellectual pursuits with work and play.

Aligning connections prevents you from losing focus and derailing your own success. The advertising industry connects with you in unconscious ways. Conscious connection is very different. When you watch a pharmaceutical commercial, you see lifestyle images of people who are happy; for them, life is easy, joyous and free. You never see a pill, a doctor, sickness or hospitals. Why? Because pharmaceutical marketers know that you don't want to connect to illness. What you want to connect with is health and a vibrant lifestyle. You connect consciously and unconsciously. When you consciously connect with your intended priorities, you can align your connections to achieve them.

The first connection you must make to be successful in the virtual workplace is with yourself. You have to be honest with yourself about your motivations, actions and intentions. The biggest obstacle you face to aligning connections in the virtual world is missing this connection with yourself. You want to define your public and your private life. It is no accident that some people succeed and others just seem to bounce from goal to goal and from career to career. Focused consciousness is powerful; unfocused consciousness is what we all are living with a great part of our lives. When you drive, you can be in a state of detached consciousness. When you surf the Internet, you can be in that same state of mind. You are there, but you are not really there.

Sometimes this is good. In athletics, it is often referred to as *the zone,* a state of awareness that is simultaneous and detached from a higher state of consciousness. When you are in the zone, you are not really thinking; doing and performance come automatically. What you don't see in reading about the zone is the hours of practice and focused concentration it took to get to that state of performance. It took a lot of concentration, focus and hard work, not to mention hours and hours of practice. If you want to make it happen in the virtual workplace, you want to connect first of all with yourself and then with everybody else.

Developing a sense of self-awareness is not an easy task. It is much easier for most of us to look critically at others than to self-examine and discover our own motivations, actions and flaws. But there is no one you will spend more time with in the virtual workplace. It is critical that you know yourself, and that you are honest about who you are and what is in your baggage.

You have the opportunity to connect with friends and family, workers and coworkers, acquaintances and the media in any number of ways. There are many ways to connect in a world driven by social media. Sometimes, you connect in ways that you are not even aware of, whether you wanted to or not. All of this connection, both wanted and unwanted, can lead to consequences. These can have a great influence on your success in the virtual workplace. Awareness first: you can't have alignment without awareness.

Motivational author and speaker Zig Ziglar (2013) said, "If you want to reach a goal, you must 'see the reaching' in your own mind before you actually arrive at your goal." Do you have the goal of being valued, respected and involved? Is that how you are aligning your connections? If you want people to see you as an integral part of the team, are you aligning your connections so that you show up and participate in virtual meetings? Do you reach out for help when you have questions? Notify your boss if the deadline is slipping? Are you intentionally kind? Are you non-confrontational -- even on Facebook? Do you meet people on fair and equal terms in a non-judgmental way?

VIRTUAL CULTURES AND COMMUNICATIONS

Become aware of your instinctual way of communicating with others. Along with personal and interpersonal connections in the virtual world, you want to be aware of cultural barriers and challenges. Culture can be defined using a multitude of topics and categories. The easiest way to define *culture* may be: what people think, feel and do. Culture can be global, it can be local, it can be corporate or it can be social. However you look at culture, it concerns values and beliefs that then play out as behaviors and interactions. When you communicate in the virtual world, you cannot assume anything. Communications is the glue that holds the virtual world together. The arsenals of technologies that are available to you are there really for just one reason: to let you communicate with other people from a distance. When you align connections, you need to convey information to others in the most expedient and efficient way possible. Why send 100 emails back and forth when a quick web conference would get the job done? You want to be conscious of the impact the technologies have on context.

We have no shortage of technologies and more are on their way. The importance of these technologies is really to help you and other virtual workers communicate and get the job done. Factual information like budget spreadsheets, sales plan presentations and production schedules are pretty straightforward. There is little ambiguity. Social information communicates attitudes and expectations as well as tangible facts. This makes it subject to interpretation and perceptions. Normally, you rely on your five senses to makes these interpretations, or maybe six if you count intuition.

When you work in the virtual workplace, you have less visibility. Others can't see you and you can't see them, not even with video – or at least not in the same way. When you walk into your virtual office, no one else is there. The office style and dress code have little meaning to a virtual team. You can be connected to each other and to another activity at the same time: faxing, emailing, conferencing and scheduling. This increased dependency on technology can cause you to feel isolated, with less social interaction and cultural affiliation. Nonetheless, you still need to make deadlines, get tasks done and adhere to other group norms and practices. Without the visual cues, expressing shared expectations and agreeing upon effective contributions becomes even more important. This can be difficult.

Observing common settings and drawing on common experiences gives us a common culture. In some offices it was commonplace to require men to wear white shirts. It may not have been a written rule, but everyone always had one on. This is unspoken communication and expressed the expectations of the group. You may or may not have received comments when you wore a blue shirt, which was explicit communication. Both written and unwritten rules of behavior still exist in the virtual workplace. The difference is you have no one to compare yourself with so you may not even know enough to ask the right questions. This is one reason that structure becomes so important in the virtual world.

The skills you need to thrive in the virtual environment are not altogether different than the ones you needed in the traditional workplace. None of the five respond-abilities will be a handicap if you have them in a face-to-face environment. However, if you do not have them in the virtual workplace, it will be much more difficult to thrive. These skills let you blend different facets of your life and get things done. The five respond-abilities help you manage the nuances of *The Pajama Effect*. Overcoming the roadblocks to your success is what this book is about. The rest of this book is dedicated to giving you not only theory and explanation but practical exercises and examples to assure your success in the virtual workplace.

4

Act with Autonomy

"Every human has four endowments – self-awareness, conscience, independent will and creative imagination. These give us the ultimate human freedom...The power to choose, to respond, to change."

-- *Stephen R. Covey*

When you were in the traditional office, you had colleagues surrounding you. You had protocols to obey and water coolers to visit. You could stop in at your buddy Joe's office to see what he thought of the latest memo from corporate. As long as you got along and went along, things went your way. If the accepted office policy was to arrive early and stay late, that is what you did. If you complied with corporate conventions and did not rock the boat you were considered a good employee. All that has changed in the virtual office. You must act with autonomy because you have no choice. In the virtual office, you are alone a great deal of the time with yourself, which can be a dangerous place to be.

Acting with autonomy is more than just being independent and self-reliant. It is the ability to carry through with your own agenda. To act with autonomy, it is critical you learn to think with autonomy; this is always the first challenge for the virtual worker because you are missing the feedback of visible cues. The virtual environment is two-dimensional and farther removed. Not only do you not have visual cues, you do not have emotional cues, either. There is so much more to interpret and so much more room for interpretation.

When you act with autonomy, you are confident that you have the skills to get the job done. You may not have all the resources, but you know how to access them. This also means that you understand the company's goals and conduct your daily responsibilities in accordance with the company's vision. You may not agree with every detail, but you are there to perform to the best of your abilities. In the virtual office, you will sometimes be put on the spot, and you will be pushed to make a decision about an issue or take action. You will not always have the opportunity to call your boss or your colleague and ask what they think. You will have to make the decision at that moment and take responsibility for your actions. You are more autonomous because you cannot walk over to anyone's desk while the client is on hold. You are better able to act with autonomy when your actions are grounded in the company's business vision.

LEARNING LESSONS FROM BEYOND THE CUBICLE

Being able to track your own agenda starts with an awareness of where you are and how the virtual world is very different. You have more freedom but much less wiggle room, as the digital world is more unforgiving and it never really forgets. In the cubicle, your identity was pretty well defined. The organizational and social structures of home, family and play were set by rigid rules related to your role at work: time, schedules and corporate rules.

We have come a long way since the days of Freud's cynical theories that we were led by unknown forces and had little influence over our conscious autonomy. Radical individualism has been with us since Emerson wrote his essay, "Self-Reliance." It is an American value that is instilled in our culture and social systems. For decades, we have had a safety net in the workplace because we only had to be partly independent. We had the company and we had each other to reinforce what was acceptable, what was necessary, and what was to be done and when. We had conformity: we dressed alike, we worked 9-to-5 and we "drank the corporate Kool-Aid." It is what we did if we wanted success. The existentialists may have been right, but it wasn't anything we had to concern ourselves with. We were all linked in similar ways and we reinforced each other.

When we moved from the cubicle to the virtual office, all of that changed. The rules of 9-to-5 became 24/7. We became invisible and in charge of our own destinies. There is no one there to watch us, judge us or control us. We are alone with ourselves and uncomfortable. Anxiety, stress, and anger all come with us. All the parts of our conscious and subconscious minds, what Freud called the ego and id, moved out of the cubicle and into an environment so new, so strange and so different that we really do not know how to handle it. The expectations are still there; in fact, they are greater than ever before but the constraints are gone. The boundaries and limits have been removed. We are more vulnerable yet must be more disciplined. Most importantly, we are expected to produce results.

Competition is out; *collaboration* is now the favorite buzzword. We have social networks to chat on and video to chat with. We have the freedom to do a load of laundry in the middle of the day and the responsibility to meet our workplace deadlines just the same. It is much harder to compare ourselves to everyone else because we cannot really see them. Our accomplishments became our own responsibility. We have to get up, figure it out and move forward one step at a time toward our goals, on a daily basis. We need inspiration from within or intrinsic motivation. But what we get are distractions of all sorts: dogs barking, phones ringing, washers beeping, children crying, doorbells chiming and delivery people knocking. We have to manage our professional life in a different way because it is now taking place right alongside our personal life. There are no more walls and no more segmentation or isolation between our identities.

Intrinsic and Extrinsic Distractions

Workplace success in this environment depends on your ability to manage internal and external distractions. In some ways, the UPS delivery person, the barking dogs, the toddler and the cleaning person are the easy things to manage. It is your thoughts and your emotions, those things that internally distract you from your tasks, that are often more difficult to manage. Self- governance means more than it did in the cubicle. It means controlling your environment, your schedule and your thoughts. You need to stay on the positive side of things and keep your box open at the top.

How autonomous are you? Sometimes you will follow the rules and other times break them. You want to know your company's protocol. There has been a lot of initiative in the last few years to teach organizations innovation and creativity, to "think outside the box." But can you really do that? Can you think beyond your own consciousness or your own knowing? First, you need to be aware of what you are thinking and then focus your thoughts so that you are on the positive side of things. You need to stay focused and be intrinsically inspired. If you are going to "think outside the box" then your box needs to be open at the top. The term implies doing something differently, expanding beyond what is normal and pushing your limits. Your perspective is your box and it is unrealistic to ask people to think outside of the box. You have the ability to learn something new; when you learn, you get a bigger box. No one will give you a bigger box; you must create it yourself. The box is your mind, your thought processes. Any limitations, you create for yourself. Knowledge and awareness are the contents of your box. Research in the last decade or more on cognitive behavior therapies – from people such as Aaron Beck, David Burns, Albert Ellis and Martin Seligman – has shown the importance of having positive thoughts.

In the virtual environment, you are constantly being pulled or pushed. Internally, you have your own inspirations and certain ideas attract your attention. They usually lead to positive feelings or emotions. On the other hand, you may be externally pushed to do more with less, to stay up late in order to meet with a colleague, to work extended hours today because you went to the beach yesterday and did not do what you had to do.

The external push and the internal pull can create conflict for you. So, to act with autonomy, you want to find a balance, feel confident about what you are doing and still satisfy your job requirements. When you work from home, anything can be a distraction. Your parent, child, spouse, neighbor, mail carrier, neighbor's lawnmower – the list goes on and on. When you find out what distractions are around you, minimize them.

You are responsible for creating your own work environment. What you bring to that environment is important to your ability to be successful within that environment. You probably don't have any company policy about how to decorate your office. You certainly are not confined to a cubicle. You may use a beanbag for a chair, work from your sofa or outside in the garden. The office can be whatever you want it to be. It can be relaxed and optimistic or stressful and pessimistic.

The effects of this environment are exaggerated because our method of communicating in this work environment is not face-to-face. You are free to create an atmosphere that best suits you. The virtual environment does not have the same visual cues or the same intuitive interpretations. You are more subjective and you are more strongly influenced by your own thoughts and emotions. You filter things differently in the virtual world.

A communication or interaction may be distorted by: taking it personally, making assumptions, jumping to conclusions, fortune-telling, blowing things out of proportion, acting on shoulds and musts, overgeneralization, and labeling (Burns, 1999). All of these filters that distort thinking and put you in a negative place in the face-to-face world are still present in the virtual environment only they are more exaggerated. Why more exaggerated? – because in the virtual environment, we are more alone with ourselves.

One way to counteract the tendency to be negative is to focus on what inspires you. By reframing things in a positive manner you can influence your own success. Everyone has a source of inspiration. Ask yourself: What is yours? When you find your source of inspiration, you will be more open to new things because you can then look at the world through the lens of positivity. Your ideas may be crazy, perfect, good, cool or even duds. Be open-minded and keep yourself inspired.

Starting new positive thought patterns is much easier than trying to change old negative ones. It is easier to concentrate on starting to eat healthy than on stopping the consumption of junk food. It is easier to stay on task instead of fixing procrastination, or learning to be relaxed instead of conquering your stress. Changing your thoughts requires that you first become aware of them. How you talk to yourself and how you speak to others makes all the difference in the world. Changing your communications to be positive, upbeat and supportive is especially important in the virtual workplace. Make some effort to focus on "what is" and spend less time on "what is not." This will help with the internal distractions and distorted thinking, and let you build a positive attitude. Your perspective on your ability to do a good job and make things happen will help you be successful without a cubicle or corporate structure.

NO COLLABORATION WITHOUT AUTONOMY

In the virtual world, the field of play is more level and the trappings of hierarchy have been removed. There are no more corner offices, head chair at the conference table or executive restrooms. You have a much greater hand in creating your own destiny. Your personal identity – how you think about yourself – plays an important role. It includes the self-appraised characteristics you think you have, including your strengths and weaknesses. The virtual worker has the ability to not only individuate, a term Jung used to describe the development of the perceived self, but also to de-individuate or go beyond the limitations of the self because of the unique characteristics of the environment. Virtual workers need to have a conscious connection to their own thoughts and abilities to get results.

Personal identity affects everything the individual does. If you do not believe you can do something, whether because of a lack of confidence or a negative attitude, you will struggle in the virtual world. Because so much is hidden online, you can have a sense of dissociation, disinhibition or deindividuation (Suler, 2004). This means we do, say and act in ways that we would never dream of in a face-to-face environment. This can be positive or negative. Quite often it is filled with contradictions.

We have all read stories about close intimate relationships people develop online only to find out later that the commitment was not mutual and left one person feeling vulnerable and exposed. The online world lets us hide some or all of our identities. Online, it is easier to feel a degree of separation from our actions and their consequences. Our online psyches are more removed and detached than in a face-to-face situation. People go places and do things under the pretext of anonymity. Even if people know who you are, you do not have the same kinds of interactions as you do when you can shake hands, read facial expressions and watch gestures. We react differently when we interact online.

We feel lost emotionally when we are without external cues from other people. Much of our fitting in comes from our reactions to approval and disapproval. These social norms and standards are interrupted in an environment where interactions can be hours or even days apart. Because we do not have to deal with immediate approval or disapproval in the virtual world, we are less influenced by the expressions of others and more influenced by ourselves (Baggio & Beldarrain, 2011). Our internal thoughts, feelings and boundaries, both benign and toxic, are more likely to come out. People feel safe saying and doing things they never would say or do face-to-face. And when we sign off, we can let it go, as if that part of us is no longer important. This newfound freedom supports revealing personality quirks, emotional attributes and self-identity. This varies with role-playing, experimentation and multitasking. There is probably not one online other self, but several (Turkle, 2012).

These self-centered disinhibitions make collaboration even more difficult in many cases. Collaboration in virtual teams and the social networks is often a fantasy. Self-centered attitudes and disinhibitions may serve the self but not take the needs of others into consideration. Yet online independence has to reflect more than just achieving your own goals and desires. Independence has to mean thinking and behaving in a way that meets your own requirements but also takes others into consideration. You have to be independent enough to look at what you are thinking and realize how that is being interpreted in the virtual world.

We have all had an email taken the wrong way. We have all experienced someone's temper when the meaning was truly and totally benign. Independence here is the ability to stop automatic thoughts and be aware of how your behavior is being interpreted by others. This includes being aware when your own interpretations of others are exaggerated, biased or just wrong. Once you become aware of your own independent thoughts, you can begin to interact successfully with others.

Collaboration is about trusting each other enough to open up and share our talents in order to achieve something. When we are trying to achieve something, we can put ourselves under stress and when we are stressed we can revert to old behavior patterns that may no longer serve us. This is why the ability to act with autonomy is so important for successful collaboration.

FLEXIBILITY AND FOCUS

Freedom and flexibility are two of the most beneficial aspects of being a virtual worker. You have the freedom not only to create your own dress code, but also to flex your hours. For example, if you go to a doctor's appointment in the morning, you know that when you return you must make up the lost time. You also have the freedom to check your emails on your smartphone and use the time spent in the waiting room productively. This might save you time later. In the virtual workplace, you are the boss of your time. You have more flexibility and freedom but also have more responsibility.

Many people have trouble adapting to this. It requires confidence to get back on track when one is temporarily pulled off. You have to be confident in your own abilities to get things done and to achieve results. If you struggle with low self-efficacy, you are going to have a hard time in the virtual workplace. All sorts of factors can sidetrack you, most typically: excuses, procrastination and self-criticism.

Excuses are a way to give yourself permission to not do what you know you need to do to get the job done. They release you from responsibility and give you a way to blame conditions or other people. Excuses give you a way of providing an explanation for your behavior or someone else's. Psychologically, you are off the hook or have, at least, created the appearance of acceptability and less offensiveness. Some people become so good at this and so creative that they actually start to believe their own reasoning. These excuses can become really creative in the virtual world because you have the guise of invisibility. No one really knows if your excuses are true; you have no witnesses.

Let's take a look at excuses and see how they fit in your box. Excuses in the digital world come in all shapes and sizes. Some are so common that they are worth listing here for you. Do any of these sound familiar:

> "There is something wrong with the technology. It doesn't work, it is down, it doesn't function the way it should, the power is out, the time is different, the sound doesn't work, the reception is bad…whatever…the technology has let me down. I cannot accomplish what I am supposed to accomplish and it is not my fault. It is the fault of the technology. I blame the technology for my failure or my inability to do what I said I was going to do; therefore, I am off the hook."

"I am having personal life difficulties. My child, parents, spouse, neighbor, contractor or friend is making my life uncontrollable. I cannot do or accomplish or live up to what I said I would accomplish because these people are infringing on my time. I have to do something else because of them and that is forcing me to be unable to live up to the commitment I made. They are the problem, not me, because they distract me."

"I cannot complete what I said I would do, or attend the meeting or class I said I would attend. I cannot get the report to you or complete the agreed-upon task on time because some other aspect of my work has taken over my time, life or ability to get this done. I just took on a new client and I am swamped, I got a new assignment and that takes up all my time, I am traveling more now, you know…I am in a new position and I have more responsibility that I did so I cannot get it done, my plate is too full. It is not my fault; my other work is to blame for my inability to deliver this project on time."

"I am in some way hindered by an illness, accident, ache, pain or incapacity that has to do with my physical health. I have migraines, stomach trouble, back problems, a cold, the flu, insomnia or a sprained ankle. I am physically incapable of doing what I said I would do; therefore, I am off the hook. I can't help it if I am sick, injured or out of commission. Not my fault."

"I just don't have time. I am so busy; it is overwhelming. I underestimated the amount of time it takes to study, read, prepare, meet online and participate. I didn't take into consideration that I have three children, ages four, six and eight at home and that working from home would require time. I am not sure where the time goes. I get up early and I put a lot of time into this and I just never seem to get it done. It just takes up so much time. It's not my fault there are only 24 hours in a day."

"This is not what I thought it would be. My perception of working remotely was very different than what it actually is. I miss the office talks, the people and the conversations. I thought this was going to be something and it turned out to be something different. I don't like it, I feel uncomfortable. It is not my fault that I am not successful at it. It isn't what I expected and, therefore, I am not responsible for not being successful."

Procrastination can be so strong that even if you know you are going to miss the deadline, not hand in the assignment or blow the deal, you will still procrastinate. There is a great deal written about procrastination and resistance. Procrastination is something we will talk about at length later in Chapter 6, Be Authentically Productive. For now, let's just say that, most of the time, procrastination results from low self-efficacy and it impedes your productivity. There's usually some emotional baggage incorporated in as well that may date back to childhood (Natural Remedies for Total Health, 2013).

Self-criticism is another emotional and psychological state brought on by negative thoughts. The source of this can go back to childhood and haunt people into adulthood. If you don't get a handle on what you say to yourself and how you say it, a lot of emotional damage can be done and inspiration lost.

Since the arrival of positive psychology, much work has been done on discovering your personal strengths. By emphasizing your strengths instead of your weaknesses, you will feel you have the power to accomplish more in your life. You need to feel that you call the shots in your life and control your own destiny. While positive belief and self-efficacy are important for everyone, these thought systems are essential for the virtual worker. Because you spend so much time alone with yourself, it is important to pay attention to what you say to yourself. It is easy to take things personally or out of context in the virtual world. You assume everything reflects on you. Negative internal chatter creates a more isolated and negative environment. Because of the lack of cues and feedback from others, virtual workers have to work a little harder to make sure that what they think is happening is real.

Using emoticons or including extra phrases like "virtual smiles" or "thumbs up!" help to set the tone of messages and texts. All conversation, especially when the cues are removed, is subject to the perception of the individual. Staying in a positive frame of mind and being aware of what you are thinking and saying to yourself is paramount if you are going to act with autonomy.

Interestingly, this is the exact opposite of what many of us have been taught to do. For most of us, social norms and education mores taught us to comply: Raise your hand if you want to speak; stay in line. This was great training for conforming but not for autonomy. In the virtual workplace, creativity and spontaneity are important. You have the ability to create your own schedule, focus on your goals and meet them. Virtual workers struggle with having no more conformity, order and control because that is what they have been taught most of their lives. The limits, boundaries and restrictions came from others. With those removed, you have to put a conscious effort into how you make use of your new freedom and flexibility.

The rhetoric of rugged individualism has been a part of certain political components in the U.S. since pre-colonial days. Unfortunately, society and the media have done little to help us truly establish ourselves as independent identities. Real autonomy is important. The virtual worker has the opportunity to redefine identity on a much more level playing field. You can define yourself without the visual cues and social inequalities of the cubicle. You can also participate in many things unobserved and change your perspective more easily, although in the digital world there is ongoing, recorded testimony of who you are. Personal and social identities are defined not only by us but also by others for us as well. Real autonomy starts with your ability to think and act for yourself.

Your ability to collaborate on virtual teams and interact with others will be greatly influenced by your ability to act with autonomy. Identity with the collective whole will be more difficult if the expected behaviors, role relationships and interactions are based on dependency and not collaboration. Your ability to act with autonomy is wrapped up with your belief in your ability to reach goals and produce results to meet the expectations of your employer and yourself. Autonomy allows you to have a strong sense of self but also a sense of assimilation with your company, organization and co-workers.

New, better and integrated technologies are supporting the virtual worker, yet technologies alone are not enough. Acting with autonomy means thinking and behaving in ways that support you in achieving your own agenda. New communications tools are helping support new types of community integration with others. Acting with autonomy aligns facts, explanations, goals, actions and reasoning with your own personal objectives. It produces results that make you happy, your boss happy and your friends and family happy, too.

THE ABILITY TO ACT

Because we are social beings, the virtual environment can often feel dehumanizing, disconnected and stressful. Only when we learn to take positive actions will we be able move forward successfully. There are many potential reasons why humans react instead of responding to a situation. It may have to do with how you are wired, your conscious awareness and your prior experiences. There are really two parties connected to your success in the digital environment: you and others (Kahneman, 2011).

When you are exposed to something new and different you may experience a difficult adjustment period. The digital workplace brings about behavioral and psychological changes. In the right light, the changes should be seen as positive. The virtual worker can juggle the environment and all the different responsibilities. Difficulties may arise from fear, frustration, or lack of something such as knowledge or time. Any of these may be the reason why you might find yourself reacting instead of acting. Self-reflection is a powerful tool; in the virtual environment you are your closest ally. Self-reflection is something you can use as a tool to help you move forward.

Fear is a dangerous and powerful emotion. It has its place as a warning mechanism but can wreak havoc if not curtailed. You may fear the unknown because you are not sure if you will like this new way of work, are not sure where to set up your laptop or know what kind of desk to purchase. You may be afraid of being bored, lonely or lost. You may even be afraid of how this new way of working fits into your family life. Even if you live alone, you may fear how to make it all work or you may fear how others may view your new situation. You may ask yourself: "Will they laugh? Will others take me seriously as a professional? Will this new way of work interfere with my ability to get a promotion? Can I really do this?"

Instead of pulling yourself together and strategically planning your new workstation, or candidly talking to your friends and family about your new way of work, you may find yourself making up excuses for not buying a desk, re-organizing your priorities or focusing on your new freedom. You might be in danger of losing sight of your purpose and sinking into depression. You might be secretly hoping that this is just a bad dream and, in the morning when you wake up, you can drive to the old familiar office building.

Fear can quickly lead to frustration or anger if you don't know what to do about it. You may be an excellent salesperson but suddenly you feel inadequate, as if you lack the skills to organize your day and focus on work. Maybe you suddenly feel a lack of personal time and feel tied to technologies around the clock. Frustration is likely to peak when there are pressures from family and friends who are not used to seeing so much of you. Let's face it: this new environment is also a change for them. They may unconsciously expect you to be more available just because you are physically there.

There may also be pressure from your boss who has not been trained to manage remote employees. Chances are that your supervisor is as lost as you are; therefore s/he is making unrealistic demands of you and may be equally frustrated. Maybe your boss wants to keep tabs on you at all hours of the day, and you feel compelled to say "yes" to each and every demand. Whether this pressure is real or perceived, the effect is the same. You will react in ways that can cause you to perform at less than your best. When you are under pressure, you may react by ignoring those who need your attention or by not giving your attention to those who should truly have it. You do things halfway because you are pressed to do the next item on the list. Maybe you forget about the list altogether and only get to the first item. You react and seek refuge in unproductive activities that do not necessarily allow you to relax.

You were busy but not getting things done. You aren't really sure what happened to all the time and suddenly the day is over. Your priorities are out of order and your life is out of balance. It makes you resent this new way of work even more. It's not only your way of work that has shifted, but also your personal life and your priorities. What can you do? How can you get the right perspective? How can you conscientiously act in ways that lead you to success? A good start is to accept the effect the virtual environment can have on you, the organization you work for and the society in which you live.

BLURRING THE LINES AND DEFINING SUCCESS

The Pajama Effect has redefined our idea of success and what it means to be a productive employee. Your contribution level, as an individual, is more important than ever. Organizational success is now a bottom-up phenomenon. Institutional structures are falling away, replaced by a workplace where collaboration and contribution are praised and rewarded. Formalized structures are being eliminated and new social communications allow for more horizontal and equal contributions. Collaboration has long been recognized as a critical component for business success. The truth is, most people are not very good at working alone. You need other people and they need you.

You need these other people because you are human. Dependence means you change your state of being and act or react based on what others do. You are conditioned from childhood to react to others. Interdependence means the quality or condition of being mutually reliant on each other. Collaboration helps virtual workers pick up on changes in the workplace and changes in mutual awareness. Intrinsic inspiration leads to independence and autonomy. Independence and autonomy, in turn, lead to success. Steve Covey says you go from being dependent to independent, and then to a state of interdependence. This is one reason why acting with autonomy is so important in the digital world. Collaboration with others is imperative, but to collaborate it is essential for you to act with autonomy. This requires a sense of self-reliance, self-sufficiency and self-governance (Covey, 1989). In the digital world, it is way too easy to close yourself off.

When organizations implement new processes that include virtual teams or remote employees of any kind, their leaders must take proactive measures to create a support system for these workers. The support system can include technology support but must also support the human connection. Very few organizations have a proven method of training and supporting virtual employees or a method for leading and managing them. This opens the door to a Pandora's Box of problems, because a leader cannot lead the virtual worker if that worker does not understand what it is that helps achieve success. It used to be when you worked, you worked, and when you played, you played, but those lines are blurring. Blurred lines make it more difficult to define success.

You can show up physically but not mentally. More often than not, people partially show up. They may be physically connected to work, but not engaged or attentive emotionally, not fully present. It is easy to disengage, to hit the "mute" button and go change the laundry, feed the dog or make lunch. You may feel free to act and do things that you would never do in the office. You comb your hair or pick your teeth. You are physically present, but mentally distracted.

Driven by cheap connectivity, virtual meetings and conference calls have become the norm. No one is really sure what the correct and ethical protocol is when meeting in the pajama world. Because communicating in the virtual workplace involves anonymity, miscommunication is one of the biggest challenges you face. You want to be able to think, manage and inspire yourself. This is nothing new: humans have been doing it for an eternity. On the farm, things were done creatively in a self-reliant, self-inspired atmosphere. Even in the age of hunter-gatherers, humans had to be flexible and inventive. It wasn't until the transformation of the agrarian age into the industrialized age that we went from creative jobs to thoughtless rote jobs that lacked spontaneity.

With *The Pajama Effect* you are psychologically in a more vulnerable state. Think about being in your pajamas. How do you feel? You are alone or at least in the company of a few comfortable friends or family members. You are more open, more susceptible to being seen just as you are. You are more exposed to your own idiosyncrasies and excuses. You do not have on your work persona and have not dressed in the related armor – either physically or psychologically – to do battle in the outside world. The lines between public and private, work and play, home and the office, are blurred.

You are a bit more sensitive both to external and internal influences. This vulnerability is influenced both by the potential impact of an event or situation and the adaptive capacity of the person. If the technology goes down, what do you do? Do you go to a coffee bar, the library or your neighbor's house? Do you borrow a computer from the kids, go to the local high school or call a friend? Or do you just say, "I can't or won't adapt. This is an outside influence and there is nothing I can do to change the situation." In the digital workplace, you are free to handle things or not. It is your choice to take the initiative and try to rectify the situation, make adjustments and realign priorities. You can choose to be relaxed and more productive, or tense and less productive. You create the atmosphere you could not create in the company cubicle farm. You can't blame things on anyone or anything else.

Do things happen in digital workplaces that are out of your control? Of course they do. It is not what happens that is important, but it is your ability to respond, not react, and your actions that will influence the positive or negative outcome. So, be in charge of your actions, make the best of each situation and change your thinking to what supports your success.

BOUNDARIES, SYMBOLS AND INFLUENCES

Your success is influenced by more than just your conscious intentions; it also is profoundly influenced from the subconscious mind. For the purposes of this book, I will put everything below the surface of consciousness into a category called "subconscious" and not distinguish between the personal subconscious, the collective subconscious and the unconscious mind. If something is not part of conscious thought, then I consider it subconscious and below the surface of consciousness.

Let's go back to the physical office for a second. When you were in a traditional work environment, were there company logos on all the floors, in the lobby and on the doors? On the notebooks, windows and murals? On the company letterhead or the digital template? What is a company logo anyway? It is a symbol and symbols have a very strong influence on the subconscious mind.

When you see the Nike swoosh logo, what do you think of? If you answered, "Just do it" and Nike, you are absolutely right. But don't stop there. There is a lot more meaning attached to that little figure than just a few words. Once you are aware of this meaning, it is always in your subconscious even if you simply say it means Nike. Otherwise, why would we pay so much money to wear Nike shoes? Or why would there be million-dollar lawsuits over the ©? Why do people protest and riot over the peace sign? It is just three little lines in a circle. Why would you want to go to jail over that?

It is much easier to be limited by boundaries when they are already set in your conscious and subconscious. The environment you are in molds and shapes you; it conditions your reactions. Boundaries provide unwritten expectations for behaviors. Walls, roles, functions and the environment set the physical boundaries. In the mailroom, they sort the mail, and in the conference room, we conference. There are lines drawn both consciously and unconsciously about what you can do in each room. There are logos on the wall and pictures on the boss's desk. When you are in the boss's office you act, communicate and confirm that you are interacting with the boss. The virtual world's boundaries and symbols can act as border restrictions and limits; some of these are already set for you because you physically are where you are.

In the traditional environment, connection boundaries were set by whom you worked with and where you worked. A little personal communication was probably acceptable but too many personal calls were considered behavior that was not on task. You knew these boundaries and you adhered to them. The expectations were clearly defined, either in a spoken or written policy, or implied by the unspoken word. Time and space were also well defined in the traditional work environment. You worked 9-to-5 or 12-to-7. You went to work and when you clocked out, you were no longer expected to be on "company time." You didn't bring your parents, your children or your dogs into the office.

Why not? You didn't do it because it was company space. If you are going to be efficient, you must stay on task. Being on task and reaching a standard of high performance means you have to concentrate or focus on what it is that you want to accomplish.

Functioning with *The Pajama Effect* means blurring these lines, limits and boundaries. It means the company no longer sets up the boundaries, or at least not all of them. You do. It means a blending and blurring of expectations, emotions and behaviors. All of these have to be managed and executed in a way that ultimately leads to your success. You must conscientiously decide to take proactive measures to keep yourself organized and focused, but also sane in the ever-challenging virtual office. The blending of your private world with the demands of the virtual workplace requires you to take responsibility and care.

We all come to the planet with special gifts and talents. We have natural abilities to perform. Our insights, instincts and independence can be (and often are) trained out of us in a very systematic and powerful way. We are influenced by our family of origin, the educational system, religious affiliations and society at large. The age of media has intensified this subconscious programming. We are constantly performing to the expectations of others. This tends to remove us from our own sense of inner independence. We become more interested in people-pleasing and not making trouble than in our own autonomy. So, the first step in responding with autonomy is to get in touch with who you really are, what you love to do and how you can support yourself. We all need food, shelter, acceptance and love. We are social and connected beings by nature.

Meet Brad

Brad is a freelance writer and a very intelligent man. He has been working as an independent consultant for years. He is in his early 50s and recently reunited with his ex-wife. Until recently, Brad always went into a client's office, where he had support, boundaries and structure provided by the organization. Brad became a graduate student in an online program and struggled mightily with getting things done. He would disappear for weeks at a time, not making deadlines for postings and assignments. He always had an excuse: he was too busy at work, new assignments had come up, the computer was acting weird, his Internet was giving him trouble or his daughter needed a ride somewhere. It was always something. Brad was not getting the results that he wanted or that his program demanded. Procrastination, excuses and negative thinking would always get the best of him. He wasn't getting the job done. He kept falling back into old patterns of justifications, letting himself off the hook by blaming everything and anything except himself. Brad became convinced that working in the virtual world just wasn't for him and that he missed other people. But was it really other people he missed? Why? Brad was not pleasing anyone, especially himself. What do you suggest to help him adjust to "Acting with Autonomy?"

106

Meet Tracy

Tracy is a college senior who was lucky enough to secure a job working with an ex-assistant Secretary of State, helping her do the research to write a book. Tracy, an excellent student, college athlete and self-starter had never worked in the virtual environment before, nor had her employers had much experience managing virtual employees. She was used to performing at a high level but with the help of physical surroundings and peers who supported her and provided structure. At the beginning of the summer, when Tracy first started her job, she would go to Starbucks to work. Even though she had connections, fast Internet access and everything she needed right at home, it was difficult for her to focus and concentrate. By changing the physical environment, much like going to a library to study, she was able to get down to working and get things done.

Over time, this effect began to lessen and she became used to working virtually. She created a space for herself that was her workspace, bought herself a new computer and set up shop. She developed a schedule where she had structure and order. She started at a certain time and ended at a certain time, daily. During this time, the television was off and the cell phone mostly unplugged. She created goals and milestones for what was productive and then made sure that on a weekly basis she met those milestones. After about three months, this was not only normal but she began to realize how much she was really getting done. She found she was much more productive in much less time than in a face-to-face situation because she could focus her energy on the task at hand. She had the internal and behavioral skills to enact self-discipline and structure and create her own routine, so she was able to make it work well. Both Tracy and the Secretary of State were happy with the results -- which is what is important in the results-oriented virtual world.

What did Tracy do that helped her succeed in the virtual environment? How might that help you or someone on your team?

Meet Susan

Susan decided to start working from home because she has a 1-year-old son and she does not want to put him in day care. Besides, she enjoys spending time with him and caring for him. Susan works full time for a software developer and her job requires her to attend weekly virtual meetings with her teammates, who also work remotely. During the virtual meetings, the group often discusses important issues about the latest projects, so it is important that everyone pays attention and offer input. Susan believes she is very good at multitasking. Right before a meeting starts, she is quick to put a load of laundry in the washer and prepare little Tommy's bottle. She is organized and feels good about working from home. The more comfortable Susan feels about multitasking, the more challenges she takes on. Just the other day, however, Susan received a complaint from a colleague who said her input was minimal and, therefore, she was no longer helpful to the team. She was shocked. Her colleague also complained that on several occasions the group could not focus on the meeting because they could hear little Tommy making noises or crying in the background. How can Susan act with autonomy to blend her private and professional lives?

RESPOND-ABILITY EXERCISES: ACT WITH AUTONOMY

Exercise 1: Who are you?

Write down the five most important things that define you.

In this exercise, write down what comes to your mind immediately. Take no more than 90 seconds to do this exercise.

Exercise 2: What do you value?

Write down five to seven things you value most.

In this exercise, write down what comes to your mind immediately. Take no more than 90 seconds to do this exercise.

Exercise 3: What do you think is expected of you?

Write down five people from your past/present and what they want or wanted FROM you.

In this exercise, write down what comes to your mind immediately. Take no more than three minutes to do this exercise.

Exercise 4: The Courage to Change

If I could make one change right now, today, to improve my life what would it be?

In this exercise, write down what comes to your mind immediately. Take no more than 10 seconds to do this exercise.

Exercise 5: Who has impacted your life? What did they do and why were they important to you?

Write down five people who have had an important impact on you and why they were important to your life.

In this exercise, write down what comes to your mind immediately. Take no more than two minutes to do this exercise.

Exercise 6: What do you love to do?

Write down five activities you love to do.

In this exercise, write down what comes to your mind immediately. Take no more than 90 seconds to do this exercise.

Exercise 7: The Evening News

If you had to go on the evening news and tell the world something that was important to you, what would you say? What would your message be? Prepare a two-minute speech. This is an elevator speech – concise, clear and deliverable. Take no more than five minutes to do this exercise.

Acting with autonomy is all about being independent and taking action. Unfortunately, for most of us this is not second nature. Fortunately, this can be learned, like all other respond-abilities. These are skills that you can acquire. If you have trouble with any of these exercises – that's good. It means you have touched upon something you may want to address. Ask yourself why it was difficult. What is stopping you? Try it again tomorrow and then the next day. Acting with autonomy requires being very secure and accepting of who you are right now. It also requires a willingness to work on what you want to change.

5

Set and Enact Priorities

"Action expresses priorities."

-- Mahatma Gandhi

There are a million courses on how to get things done, maybe more. There are many books, videos and other self-help classes available. Most of these are concerned with setting goals, making and managing to-do lists, labeling and categorizing obligations and intentions. Unfortunately, most of these are worthless. Setting priorities and carving them out requires confidence, creativity and courage. There is no right or wrong way and no quick fix for setting and enacting priorities.

This is especially true in the virtual world, where we are more open, more exposed and more vulnerable in many ways. This vulnerability is heightened by the rate of change we are all being exposed to with new technologies. We are all in a new place and working in a brand new way. Anonymity and the veil of perceived privacy also compound this vulnerability. Make no mistake – we are all in this together. Judy Brown, a mobile learning strategic analyst, told a conference at the University of Wisconsin, "We are in the first second, of the first minute, of the first hour, on the first day, of the first year" of online existence (Brown, 2012).

VULNERABILITY

Vulnerability is the feeling of being helpless, exposed and susceptible. When you put on your business suit and went to the office, you had on your business armor. This persona protected and insulated you from the dangers of being you. You became the company man or woman. You could put on another identity and became that tough businessperson, less affective and more competitive. But now that you are working in your pajamas, that business persona might look different. How much it has changed depends on you.

Your vulnerability depends on how sensitive you are to events, other people, colleagues and outside forces, and how good you are at setting your own boundaries. It also depends on how much exposure you have to risk and how much support you have from your organization. Sensitivity and exposure determine how potentially vulnerable you are to outside influences, others, family situations and distractions. Your ability to manage these by setting and enacting your priorities will determine to a large extent your ability to thrive in the virtual world.

The ability to manage your vulnerability, and adapt, helps you minimize the impact of risk and change. How you interact and share with others in the virtual world often is determined by your involvement with a team or community. Virtual communities, large or small, are places where people share knowledge, build appreciation and find opportunities. They are places to exchange ideas and information, and to seek recognition and support. Like all communities, they have a hierarchy of peer-to-peer, as well as boss/teacher-to-peer interactions and relationships. They are usually structured around common interests, productivity or consumption. Quite often, it is the virtual community that provides the support structure that helps you minimize risk and vulnerability online. Ironically, it is also this virtual community that can cause all of those to increase.

HITTING A MOVING TARGET

There is nothing more connected than the Internet and nothing moves faster than online. The ability to connect with others and share ideas has accelerated to new proportions. Digitally mediated communities use social software to determine the interactions and activities of the participants. This constantly moving target is difficult to pin down. It is not like a face-to-face workplace. It is different than it was yesterday and it will be different tomorrow than it is right now. In order to enact your priorities, you need to know what they are and then use desire, dedication and discipline to move toward them.

You can't live life online as a series of random acts or you will be in reaction mode and accomplish very little. Life in the virtual workplace affords you the opportunity to examine your desires, needs and priorities. You cannot change a global interconnected world, but you can choose how you respond to it. You can choose to state your priorities and act on them. You can become conscious of what you desire and when you want it, and focus your attention on that outcome. That is your ability to respond or "respond-ability."

In order to hit a moving target, you want to keep that target in focus. You want to aim at it until you meet your mark. It starts with an awareness of what you are trying to accomplish and then a focusing of your mind and activities on what you truly desire. Scientists used to think that our brains were hardwired and that we had very little control over what we thought and how we felt. Today we know this is not true. We have wonderful psychologists and thought leaders who tell us what we think is very important. What you think about all day long and what you do – those are your priorities.

The virtual world is always moving and most of the time you are accountable to yourself. Although some companies use conference tools and video devices to keep track of what you are doing, surveillance really doesn't work well. Most of us choose to work virtually because we appreciate the freedom. We want to be responsible enough to set our own schedule and meet the deadlines. One of the biggest changes for the pajama worker is the psychological adjustment to setting and enacting your own priorities. No more punching the clock, no more Puritan work ethic and no more playing the games. The priorities are yours and results are your results.

YOU CAN'T MANAGE TIME

You cannot manage time but you can manage you. Time just is. Depending on how honest you are and how willing you are to take charge, it is possible to determine what your priorities really are quickly. At the end of this chapter, you will find an exercise called the "You Analysis." This will help. You want to take charge of your thoughts, feelings and emotions and set your priorities. Then, once you have set these priorities, you want to apply your intent to consistently move toward them. If you are not getting what you want done and accomplishing the priorities you think you set, chances are you have another hidden agenda. You say you want one thing, but your actions say something else. The first step to changing something is being aware that it exists.

If your priority is to be a top-notch salesperson for your company, but you are not contacting your leads and making the sales calls, you are probably not going to do very well! If you are taking an online class, but you do not do the readings and participate in the group work that probably isn't going to work out so well for you, either. If you find that you set your priorities but rarely enact them, you might want to ask yourself, "Why?" If you can't easily answer that, there are literally thousands of self-help books, counseling approaches, coaches and psychologists available if you want to use them.

More often than not, you are either unaware or you have developed a to-do list that is unrealistic, overwhelming and impossible. When you don't focus on what you want, you are not going to accomplish it. When you create situations that are impossible, you are probably not going to succeed. It is impossible to go to your daughter's ballet lesson, be on the mobile responding to email, edit that report and shop for dinner all at the same time. So why do people working virtually try to do this? You didn't do it when you worked in the cubicle. You went shopping and to dancing lessons after work.

Where, once upon a time, your employer set the rules and schedule, now you have more freedom, but you still have to establish that critical path. Creating your own personal journey between waking up and going to sleep is what allows you to stay focused on your priorities and accomplish them without excessive stress, worry or fear. Setting priorities requires confidence, creativity and courage. Enacting priorities requires desire, dedication and discipline.

PERSONAL PROJECT MANAGEMENT (PPM)

Project management is all about breaking a project down into phases and activities, and applying dates and dollars to get the project done on time and within budget. Consider your life in the virtual world your personal project. Now, break it down into segments and determine what is on your priority path. Agile project management, or extreme project management (XPM), which is popular in the technical world, might be more appropriate than traditional project management for personal project management in the virtual world. Extreme project management differs from traditional project management mainly in its emphasis on open, flexible collaboration and the lack of a predetermined systematic approach. The main focus of XPM is on the results rather than on intricate scheduling techniques and heavy formalism. You can use the same approach to managing your virtual world.

You don't have to write lists as long as your arm or label everything. You won't keep this up long anyway. You can write some general things down and cross off what you have accomplished. You can write down some weekly goals and see if you meet them. You can do the same for the month and the year. You can even set a few long-term goals. These are your priorities. Then you can determine if you are moving toward them. This lets you say, "I accomplished this!" The "Your Rocking Chair Goals" exercise (pg. 133) creates awareness, both conscious and subconscious awareness. You can create vision boards, sticky note reminders, bracelets, and notecards, whatever you like. The important thing is that you do this or some variety of this and take a few minutes daily to focus on your critical path – the progress you make that moves you from where you are to where you want to be.

It takes effort, determination and some hard work to move you along this critical path. That is the dedication and discipline part of setting and enacting your priorities. But it is possible. One of the big advantages of *The Pajama Effect* is that you are in charge. You don't have to stay in the cubicle until 6 p.m. just to look devoted. You don't have to arrive at 8 a.m. because that is when the doors open. You can arrange your time and talents to optimize efficiency. That is how you set and enact priorities. You make a decision about what you want, you decide you are going to have it, and then you move in that direction by aligning your thoughts and actions with what will give you those end results (Ferris, 2009). Simple, right?

When you use personal project management, you create a specific result, or reach a milestone or deliverable. The online world never ends, so you have to establish beginning and ending points for yourself. Each day, week and month, you have things you want to accomplish. Your company or client has things that they want you to deliver. Personal project management is about timelines, budgets and resources. Just as with any project, you have to break your activities down and track them. The Project Management Institute (PMI) uses these categories for tracking projects: initiate, planning, executing, monitoring and controlling, closing. You have to begin it, plan it, do it, monitor it and finish it…whatever it is! Of course, you can break these down into many other areas. The PMI has 10 knowledge areas. You may have more or less in any of your personal or business projects.

Why is personal project management so difficult for people? Your awareness is the moving target. You react to the world around you and you lose track of your focus. In the new world, it is what you do that counts, not how much time you spend doing it. You need to accomplish results and that requires planning and focus. Here is an example: You set your priorities for health, family and work. You get up and get the coffee and sign online. You check your email and there is a coupon for Zumba lessons. Zumba is exercise and that is good for your health. You want to know a little bit more about Zumba so you Google it. You start reading the websites and watching the videos and suddenly you realize you missed the conference call you had at 9 a.m. How did that happen? You just signed on to check your email…which you still haven't really done and that was at 7:30 a.m. Now it is two hours later and you have been reading about Zumba. What happened?

You went into detached engagement. It is the same thing that happens when you drive from one place to another on automatic pilot. We have all done it. You missed the exit and you have no idea how you did that. Well, this time you missed the meeting. If you do this enough, and it is easy to do online, you will affect your work. If you value your priorities, you have to stay focused on achieving them. This begins with being aware of where you are and what is happening right now. You can only focus attention now. You can focus on the past or on the future, but you can only focus your attention now. You can prioritize activities until the cows come home, but if you don't act upon them now, you probably are not going to achieve your priorities.

If you want good health, you need to eat right, exercise and manage your vices. If you want love, you cannot go around focused on how much you hate your ex, the political candidate or the government. You can't focus on hate and get love. Which one is your priority? If you want self-expression, what are you doing to get it? Writing, painting, building, designing…there are many ways to do this. But if you are afraid to be wrong, creativity, innovation and invention are probably not happening. If you want to be a relaxed person and you run yourself ragged, you are not going to be very relaxed. Some people relax by watching movies and other people meditate under a tree. It is not important what you do. What is important is that it is your priority and you take action to move in that direction somehow. If you have your work as a priority, do the best you can at it. Show up and give it your all. If you need to get a babysitter or take the kids to day care, do it. The idea that anyone can concentrate with dogs barking, kids playing and door bells ringing is ridiculous. Outsource what you have to and focus on where you need to be.

You also will want to schedule some time to disengage from work. You cannot always be "on." If you don't schedule time to disengage, you will find that always being "on" will have a negative effect on your psychological state and your work. Psychological detachment from work during off-job times can give you high positive affect and low negative affect; that psychological detachment is particularly important when work engagement is high. A 2008 study looked at 159 employees from five German organizations, across several industries. It found that a person's level of work engagement and level of psychological detachment from work during off-job times predicted affect at the end of the workweek. The study suggests that both engagement when at work and disengagement when away from work are beneficial for employees' affective states (Sonnentag, Mojza, Binnewies & Scholl, 2008).

Finally, don't beat yourself up for not being perfect and achieving everything you want this minute. Again, there are lots of good books on this topic. Setting and enacting priorities is about valuing yourself and knowing that you can achieve what you want. You have the capabilities. There is every reason to know, recognize and understand that you can make it in this new virtual world, and be very successful. You can accept yourself right where you are and make the necessary adjustments to set and enact your priorities. With *The Pajama Effect* comes freedom; with freedom comes more fun, more flexibility and more responsibility.

BEGIN IT

To get your desired results, you have to begin. This sounds obvious, but can be a stumbling block for many people. They never start. Fear is often part of the equation: fear of failure, fear of success, fear of what others will say or not say. What is important is that you begin what you want to accomplish. A saying often attributed to Goethe states: "Whatever you can do, or dream you can, begin it. Boldness has genius, power and magic in it."

If you don't start, you can't finish. Figure out who is involved and what stake they have in the project. If your daughter needs a ride to tennis lessons, she has a stake in that event. If she is not home from being with her friends on time…well? If your company wants a report written by Friday at noon, when do they have to get you the content? Who do you have to talk to and by when? Who are the stakeholders and what do they need to know? This can be as simple as your boss, your kids or your team members. It can be as complicated as other companies halfway around the globe. Identify who has a stake in what you are doing and the results. If there are gaps in any part of this project called you, identifying them up front is very important. You might also want to identify how you will measure your success.

PLAN IT

What needs to be done and what resources do you need to do it? Analyzing what it takes to get the job done is important. Break it down and be honest with yourself and others. You can't do it all right now with no time and no resources. Create a breakout of the tasks, connections and communications, resources and budget you need. Next, determine a schedule. Create one that you will try very hard to stick to and that is realistic for you. It is important that everyone – your boss, your client, your team, and your family – be with you on the same page.

Make realistic plans, set dates and then work towards them with integrity. If you estimate some task will take three hours and you know it is at least a six-to-eight hour job, you are already behind. If you tell stakeholders up front that you need more time, you have a better chance of keeping the peace and gaining their respect. If you are always coming up short, handing things in late and making excuses, things will get old really fast. So, be realistic and honest with yourself first, and remember you need both time and resources to make plans happen. No excuses, no matter how realistically constructed, actually let you off the hook for poor planning. And planning alone is not enough, you need to monitor your progress and make adjustments regularly.

MONITOR IT

Keep track of where you are and be honest about it. Work toward your goals with integrity. It is shocking and surprising to see how many people lie to themselves. Are you communicating with people and are you making progress? If not, can you get back on track or do you need to realistically adjust the schedule? Align your connections with your goals and objectives to achieve the task you want to complete. Maybe making a chart or a list and crossing things off is helpful for you. If it is, do it. If it is not, maybe a verbal update or reflective moment will help you adjust. That is the key. When you know you are off track, do something to adjust things. You can decide to either make a change to the schedule or to your activities in order to meet the schedule.

Do not just keep rolling along, doing the same old thing, but expecting a different result. Don't count on miracles, snowstorms or guardian angels to help you get it done. Get real and be real with yourself. If you are unable to look at your behaviors honestly, admit to them and analyze where you are, you might want to ask yourself why. You may have issues you have to deal with and unrealistic expectation might be one of yours! There are lots of reasons people engage in self-sabotage. The first stage in fixing it is to realize that you are doing it. Take time to understand where you are and what you are doing well. This puts you in control of you. Monitoring progress lets you self-correct and move toward your objectives.

Integrity starts and ends with you. You can't have integrity for someone else. Integrity is an inner sense of honesty and dependability. You may judge others' integrity by holding them to a set of values, beliefs or principles they claim to hold, but all this is really external. Different societies, social groups, classes and even ethnic groups have norms that establish a kind of group consciousness where some kinds of behaviors are judged.

Companies often have cultures that support or reward honesty, dependability, kindness, creativity, etc. These are more difficult to grasp in the virtual world because the normal cues are missing, so these values and judgments must be conveyed. It is much easier to lie and conceal in the virtual environment. Distance and detachment in the online environment contribute to dishonesty. But real integrity is something that happens inside of you. It is not something that can be orchestrated. It is not situational morality. Integrity is self-honesty, self-respect and consistency in both thought and action. It is what allows you to set and enact the priorities that are right for you.

Integrity does not require observation to validate it. It does require reflection to identify inconsistencies and make adjustments. If you don't take time to look at what you are doing, you will not make the adjustments you need to make. Only you know whether you have integrity. It is much easier to judge others than to examine yourself. Integrity is a critical component in the virtual work environment. You are alone with you. You are the one you have to rely on, the one who is in control of a flexible but demanding workplace. You have freedom but responsibilities far beyond what you did in the days of the cubicle. You get to make choices and decide priorities, but with these freedoms come responsibility.

It is important the results match the expectations you have when you set and enact your priorities. You want to be satisfied and so does your employer, client or team. You want to find a way to balance work and play, family and job, productivity and relaxation, in a way that optimizes you. Integrity is about being true to yourself, your values and your priorities. First and foremost, you want to know what is important to you and you need to act accordingly.

CONTROL IT

Once you have identified where you are, you can take control of the work. If you are off schedule, this is where you get a chance to fix the schedule or what you are doing. Identifying delays and overruns early in a project is essential. You cannot set and enact priorities without being in control. Letting everybody and everything control you will result in you reacting, not responding. A great deal of this work is from the inside out. Control is often thought of as being an external thing. But the more difficult and more essential element is control over your thinking and your actions.

Because there is more freedom and fewer restrictions, both physically and mentally, in the virtual environment, it is much easier for you to lose control. Your awareness can be hijacked by distraction. The online world is loaded with distractions. Online, you have social software, emails, games, videos and a multitude of sites that entice and entrap. Offline, you have laundry, a kitchen to clean, weeds to pull, floors to wash, grass to cut and beds to make. There is no end to possible distractions as a pajama worker.

FINISH IT

You want to make sure that projects, work and play begin and end. This may be when you hand in the final report, publish the project or when the course is over. Everything needs to have a beginning and an end. Online, this is even more challenging. When you establish a schedule or a plan for your personal project, make sure you add in beginnings and endings. The virtual environment goes on all day, every day, if you don't disconnect. This is one reason so many people have a difficult time managing themselves and working effectively.

Endings are critically important for a number of reasons. Constantly repeating and ongoing projects do not give you a chance to reflect. Reflection is important to learning and appreciating what you have accomplished. This is also a stage for re-evaluation and planning what you want to accomplish next. None of this is possible without an ending.

Projects have beginning and endings. This is what makes a project what it is, a project. Even operational and maintenance tasks can have beginnings and endings. By identifying the end of a shift, a day, a particular segment or cycle, you draw a line. You create a boundary and an ending. Stopping one phase allows you to begin anew. It allows you to review the progress you have made and reflect on how you did. It provides an opportunity to determine what you might want to do differently next time. Endings allow you to free up resources, both physical and emotional, for new beginnings. Without endings, you have a tendency to stay in limbo, in- between the new and the old. In order to manage projects, even if that project is you, you want to establish beginnings and endings.

FREEDOM TO RESPOND

The road to being able to set and enact your own priorities starts with your ability to choose how you respond. You have an innate right to creative self-expression. Some of us have to overcome stronger inner bondage than others. In most cases, we can do it if we choose to grow. Being able to set and enact your own priorities starts with being ruthlessly honest with yourself. Once you eliminate blame, victimhood and other excuses (like the electricity went out) from the virtual world, you can ask yourself what is stopping you from working and leading successfully? If you feel powerless or at the mercy of others – such as your spouse, kids, employer or client – you are going to have a difficult time setting and enacting priorities. Whether you are consciously or subconsciously sabotaging yourself, you want to make the choice to figure it out.

The virtual environment requires you to develop a healthy degree of self-respect. After all, you are alone with yourself a great deal of the time. If you don't already have the capacity to take your life into your own hands, you need to develop it. You need to work on your ability to express yourself and what you want. Take time to become aware of any subconscious forces that are holding you back. Change your thinking, feeling and attitudes to ones that support you as an independent, autonomous and self-directed human being. Freedom of choice starts with a desire to be able to set and enact your own priorities. Without that desire to overcome any resistances to being in charge of you, you run the risk of getting stuck in old thought patterns, behaviors and feelings that will just not help you to succeed in the virtual environment. This is not about being self-centered or selfish. It is about being connected with what you really want and then setting off to achieve that.

The virtual world is all about connection. It is a living symbol of the collective consciousness reflected in our current society. There has never been anything like it before. It is in its infancy and, as we evolve, so will this conscious connection. Your ability to be a part of this conscious connection has accelerated dramatically in your lifetime. It doesn't matter if you are a Generation Xer, a boomer or a millennial, you have experienced the pace of life accelerating. And it is going to continue to accelerate. Nowhere is this more apparent than in the virtual environment. There is more changing here than just the increasing rate of new technologies: 3G, 4G, 5G, etc. Roles are changing, social norms are changing and values are changing, too. Working in the virtual environment brings a great many of these changes front and center. Gender roles, parenting roles and flex work are only the tip of the iceberg. Life was much simpler in many ways when everyone saw you in the office and knew you were working. You had a company identity, a private identity and a social identity; now you have a Facebook page.

Meet Kelli

Kelli is an Ivy League graduate who wanted to live at the beach, so she does. She lives and works at a beach town in New Jersey. She is intelligent, funny and very talented. She works for a social media marketing firm located in Canada. She is a self-starter and self-reliant, which works for her most of the time. The problem is that although she loves the beach and she loves her job, she struggles with meeting deadlines and loneliness. In the summer, the beach town where she lives is hopping and there is a lot to do, especially a great nightlife. In the winter, it is quiet, maybe way too quiet, and she tends to get depressed. Kelli wants more balance in her life and she wants to be able to consistently make her quotas and get her projects done on time. The president of her company flies the entire virtual staff to their Toronto headquarters a few times a year so they can meet each other and have face-to-face connections. This has been fun, but it hasn't really helped Kelli make close friends at work. Most of the time, especially in the winter, she feels pretty much alone.

Kelli's job is about connecting online. She plans, executes and monitors online media campaigns, so the last thing she wants to do is more connecting online. Her boyfriend lives in Philadelphia, about an hour away. She sees him a few times a month for a day or two. Even when she is away from work, she never feels as if she is. Kelli, like many of us, always has at least a phone or two, a tablet and a laptop with her. She loves living at the beach and really likes her job. Kelli just wants to get her job done on time, meet her deadlines and be happier. How might Kelli set and enact her priorities so she can achieve those objectives?

Meet Tariqah

Tariqah is the mother of two small children. She wants to stay at home and be with the kids during the day, so she works for a health insurance company online as a customer service representative all night. She has been doing this for

132

about four years. The pay is good, not great, and the hours are what they are. She doesn't have to pay for child care. She gets to see her children and appreciate them, when she is not totally exhausted, which she is most of the time. After working all night answering customer complaints, she gets the kids breakfast and sees them off to preschool and school. Then she lies down and sleeps until they come home. Her husband works a traditional shift and goes to a regular office. They have a fairly traditional marriage. He has a good job and makes good money. Tariqah is happy with the situation except for always being tired. She doesn't want to do this job forever because she knows it is a waste of her time and talents, as she is well-educated and has an advanced degree. For the last several years, she has been trying to plan a way out of the situation but can't seem to make much progress. She feels stuck and tired most of the time. Do you have any advice for Tariqah on setting and enacting priorities? Where do you think she is stuck?

Respond-Ability Exercises: Set and Enact Priorities

Exercise 1: You Analysis

You are going to create a job analysis for you. You will create a hierarchy, a systematic method for gathering information. You want to focus on what you do in two categories: personal and professional. Place these three areas under each category: project, play, process. Stay focused on behaviors, tasks and outcomes. Identify the personal qualifications necessary to perform your job and roles, and the conditions under which work is performed. Focus on what you do NOW or the job or role as it exists at the time of analysis; do not focus on what it was in the past, or someplace else or in the future. What do you do in these areas right now? Once you have a very detailed list, map out a day, week and month with the tasks on a calendar. What do you see? Is there an area that is dominant?

Exercise 2: Rocking Chair Goals

Picture yourself sitting in a rocking chair on a front porch when you are 116 years old. It is a beautiful day and you are looking back on your life. What five things are you glad you accomplished? These are the things that have made your life worth living. Now write five things you would like accomplish in 10 years. Next, write five things that you would like to accomplish in five years. Then write five things you want to accomplish in the next calendar year; then, five things you want to accomplish in the next six months. You should have 25 accomplishments and goals when you are finished. Take no more than five minutes to do this exercise.

When you are finished, review these exercises. Do you see a correlation, a connection, between values you include in your definition of who you are and your short- and long-term goals? Is there anything that you are doing now that is not on that list? Are you not acting in accordance with what is on the list? In order to reach your short- and long-term goals, there needs to be an alignment. The things you do in the next six months are important to those "Rocking Chair Goals." So, look at them one-by-one, review them and look for the links. Do your six-month goals align with your one-year goals? How about your five- and 10-year goals? How about your lifetime goals? This is a work in progress not a once and done activity. These are your goals and you can update and change them.

Exercise 3: What do you want to do?

Take the five six-month goals from the Rocking Chair Goals list and place them next to the "You Analysis" you created in Exercise 1. Do you see any conflicts? Mixed messages? How do you plan on accomplishing both? Does what other people want for you go against the priorities you have set for yourself?

Exercise 4: What is stopping you? What are you resisting? Why aren't you "just doing it?"

To cause real changes in behavior, you have to realize there is a good reason you are doing what you are doing. Until you identify that and quit telling yourself you are stupid, lazy, distracted or whatever, you will not change. Knowledge is not change and neither is comprehension. Behavioral and psychological change comes from application. You need to identify where the resistance is coming from and flip it. Write a list of seven activities you do for someone else. Over the next seven days, give up one of these activities each day and replace it with a priority. Remember the five activities you love. You will do or take action toward doing one of them each day for the next week.

Exercise 5: What are your priorities?

If something is stopping you from taking action, or you say one thing and do another, you need to discover why. It is not fear of failure; if you really feared failure, you would be taking steps to be very successful. It might be fear of success, or fear of a lot of things. Some people look, then leap, some people just leap, and some people look and never leap. If the latter is the case for you, at some point you gave up on yourself. You will have a very difficult time setting and enacting priorities if you don't believe you are worthy of achieving them. Starting with remembering how you felt at age five, write two sentences about how you feel and what you think you deserve. You can stop when you discover at what age you gave up on you. This will be different for everyone.

Exercise 6: Create a vision of your perfect job and the perfect day.

If you are having troubles with this, create the worst job and worst day ever. After you have created the worst day and worst job in the world, flip it. Write up to 500 words in no more than 15 minutes. If you created the situation from hell, flip those ideas one by one. Don't add anything new; just rewrite it by writing down the opposite of what you wrote for the worst scenario.

Exercise 7: Tell a vision.

Find a person you don't know and tell them what you wrote down. No negatives and no explanations why, just tell them your vision. Now tell them the five or seven things that are the most important to you. These are your priorities; because they are yours, you own them and you can always change them. The most important thing about setting priorities is that they are yours. The next most important thing is action.

6

Be Authentically Productive

"Neo, sooner or later you're going to realize, just as I did, that there's a difference between knowing the path and walking the path."

-- Morpheus, The Matrix

Ever since we adopted smartphones, we have been connected to work 24/7. These technologies can be very helpful in keeping in touch with the office, but they can also be time vampires. To prosper in the virtual world, we have to get things done. Busy is not good enough. The illusion is that we can have it all, that we can be everywhere and do everything at the same time: work, family and play. But is that really true? Or have we increased connection and not concentration? Have we developed the tools to allow us to be truly present nowhere? These technologies will keep us connected and busy, but what about productive? There are a lot of people in the virtual environment who are very busy but not authentically productive.

When you are at the soccer game, you are on a business call. When you are at work, you are sending texts to the kids. When you are out to dinner, you are checking your email. You are never truly present anywhere. No wonder you are having a difficult time staying on task. It is hard to concentrate and even harder to take a moment to reflect on what is going on. This blending of work and play should make you more flexible and fluid because the boundaries that once distinguished these separate worlds are no longer present and are not coming back anytime soon. Setting your own boundaries is extremely important to authentic productivity. But before you can set limits, you have to be aware of what you are doing. Technologies, sold as a way to stay connected, are also a way for us to disconnect from ourselves and from one another. Smartphones, online, apps and email have accelerated the pace of life. All of this connectivity does not equal productivity. In order to be productive, you need to focus.

The virtual world, though, is one of distractions. The Internet offers a wide variety of "stuff" and mobile has made it all accessible anywhere, at any time, for any reason. Bored? Just connect. You can find something that interests you. Connection, however, is not productivity. It is quite possible to be constantly connected and get nothing accomplished. In order to survive and thrive in the virtual workplace, you must learn to be authentically productive. Much of our connectivity is habit, done at an unconscious level. These technologies reinforce in us a compulsion, if not an addiction, to detached engagement. We monitor people on Facebook and feel empowered when we check email. Why? These connections stimulate our emotions and emotions are powerful. Something as seemingly benign as email has the ability to provoke love, pleasure, anxiety, even hatred. Checking your email can cause your demeanor, breathing and heart rate to change. Productivity requires you to focus that stimulation and get things done.

TIME VAMPIRES

Authentic productivity requires you to create an environment that supports you. No one is productive and creative 24/7/365. Research supports the need for a work/life balance. Creating a balanced lifestyle is about using technologies wisely. The boundaries of the workplace and workday are gone. Researchers have found that workers whose sense of self-worth and identity are closely linked to work are more likely to use technologies to stay constantly connected (Steinfield, Ellison, & Lampe, 2008). In the virtual workplace, you are free to create your own day for the most part but you still feel the pressure to be available, all the time. You may fear that if you are not always connected you will fall behind in your career, or not do a good enough job. These kinds of fears will drive you to stay connected and reconnect but maybe not for the right reasons.

Creating your own day means more than the freedom to go to the store when you want to. It also means freedom from guilt, fear and compulsion. In order to have the freedom to create an environment you want, you have to be honest and have a conversation with yourself and with your boss about what is expected and when. This is critical to working effectively in a virtual environment that spans time zones, countries and crosses continents. Even if you are in the same city, just because you can reach someone with a late night text doesn't mean you should.

If expectations are not spelled out and critical conversations discussed, then the way communication is handled is left pretty much up to the individual. Which is OK, if you are healthy, well-balanced and normal, whatever that might be. Most of us have issues of some variety or at least we know someone who does! We are all influenced to some degree by the media, the culture and society we live in and the folks we grew up around.

The idea of a work-life balance becomes even more critical when days are extended by the constant connection. Although in most cases you have the freedom to create your own work-life balance, agreed-upon expectations about when you are connected and when you need to respond help to alleviate anxiety and stress. The conversation of balance is one that needs to be addressed both by the individual and management. When an email comes in at 10 p.m., it is unreasonable to expect a reply by 9 a.m. the next day.

Connectivity is emotionally persuasive. It makes us feel important and special. Over 50 percent of us reported taking our smartphones to bed with us, 84 percent of respondents to a Time magazine survey said that they could not go a single day without their cellphones and 20 percent of respondents check their phone every 10 minutes (Gilbert, 2012). With over a billion smartphones out there, a number expected to increase to more than 4.4 billion by 2017, we have plenty of people to connect with. This connectivity gives us apparent power to choose but unless you stay aware and in charge of what you are doing it is quite possible to be very busy, yet very unproductive. It is also possible to convince yourself you are so busy, it is not your fault that what needs to be getting done isn't.

EXCUSES

We make excuses to let ourselves off the hook. We make these excuses both consciously and unconsciously. We make them for everything: deadlines, achievements and commitments. Excuses protect us from fear and from failure. They protect our sense of self and allow us to escape judgment from others and from ourselves. After all, it wasn't our fault -- right? Excuses put us in a different place. It's not that we didn't do it, we couldn't do it because…well. Excuses allow us to live with the prospect that we have the potential and we have good intentions but something, whatever, got in the way of success.

We let ourselves off the hook for not getting the project done, the assignment completed or the obligation accomplished. It is much easier to make excuses when you are detached from people. It is easier to tell a "little fib" when you don't have to look the person in the eye and lie. After all, what is the harm in it? Some of us do this so much and so often it becomes a habit. We are not consciously making excuses. But, unconsciously, we are doing it to avoid success or failure. If you neither succeed nor fail, you are in the realm of possibilities and potentialities, and that is not so bad. We have a culture that supports you 100 percent.

We do this to make the intolerable, tolerable. Rationalization sets us up to look good in our own eyes and, we hope, better in the eyes of others. We have a fear that if we are honest, others will not accept us and that is not OK. It is really not OK if we cannot accept ourselves. Rationalization is a way we deal with emotional conflict, stress or anxiety by disguising our true motivations. Our thoughts, actions or feelings are in need of explanation, so we provide one. We create an explanation that is reassuring and self-serving, but also inaccurate. We intentionally or unconsciously make up something that is incorrect.

Excuses are part of the virtual world for many reasons. For one, the speed at which this world moves causes us to experience a considerable amount of stress. When we don't manage that stress, it becomes overwhelming. We make excuses to make life easier. This becomes automatic. We are making up an excuse in our heads before we do or don't do whatever it is. We want to be treated with respect by others and we don't want to look bad. Anyone who lives online will tell you that they hear a plethora of excuses all the time! We made them to our parents and teachers and it worked.

In the virtual world where you don't have to look anyone in the eye, it is just so easy to believe they will believe you. And even if they don't, you can't see them. You can convince yourself they bought it! It is much easier to blame others and think you are not to blame when you have anonymity. The problem is, when you make excuses, you don't take charge and don't get things done. In order to survive or thrive in the virtual workplace, you and only you have to produce results. No one is there watching you.

Procrastination is a natural byproduct of making excuses. We start with the best of intentions but somehow we manage to talk ourselves out of taking action. Doubts, fears and self-judgment creep in and procrastination follows. We make excuses like, "I don't have time! What if I do it and it is not good enough? Why start if I can't do it perfectly? I don't have the energy right now! It is too much trouble!" And on and on…one excuse after another!

PROCRASTINATION

According to Psychology Today, about 20 percent of us deliberately and regularly procrastinate (Psychology Today, 2013). The isolation of the virtual environment and technologies help us distract ourselves and avoid difficult tasks pretty easily. Procrastination is nothing new. The virtual worker, however, can be even more challenged than the office worker because of the unique environment. Partially hidden and removed, the same anonymity that allows you to de-individuate will also help you procrastinate. In order to be authentically productive, you need to become more aware of what you are doing.

This sounds so easy and so obvious but it is not as simple as it sounds. You don't procrastinate because you are lazy, or because you can't manage time. The time management thing was covered in Chapter 5. You procrastinate because you have the inability to control behavior and you fail to think about thinking.

There are many studies that attempt to explain why we procrastinate. There is the 1999 study by Read, Loewenstein and Kalyanaraman which showed that we tend to pick highbrow movies but we watch the simple stuff first and somehow never get around to the ones that take a little more effort. Then there is the marshmallow study by Walter Mischel of Stanford and a host of YouTube videos that attest to the fact that self-control is not easy for about one-third of us (Mischel, Ebbesen, & Zeiss, 1972). We know this is why they have the checkout lanes stacked with gum and candy, and why, for years, you've been planning to start your diet next Monday. There are many books available on procrastination.

In the virtual world, it is even easier to procrastinate. You have an RFP (request for proposal) to write or a report to pull together, you have a paper due for class or a deadline to meet, yet here you are playing games, or folding laundry, or baking brownies. You justify this by telling yourself you will get it done. Then you go to check your email and head over to Facebook. You turn on the tube or start to watch a movie online. You just want to chill for a little and then you will get around to it. Maybe a cup of coffee will help? What are you thinking?

The truth is you are not thinking. At least you are not thinking about thinking. Thinking about thinking is what educators call metacognition. In order to think about thinking, you need to slow thought down. Much of our thinking is on autopilot. In *Thinking Fast and Slow*, Daniel Kahneman explains why the rational economic thinker is more of a myth than a reality. Human beings, it turns out, don't always think rationally (Kahneman, 2011). Some of this has to do with instinct and how we are hardwired and some of it has to do with lack of metacognition.

If you were thinking about thinking, you might realize that you have to write the report, meet the deadline or finish your part of the proposal or you may not have a job. This could be really bad because then you won't be able to have food in the refrigerator and pay the rent. But, right now, cleaning out the hall closet seems like a much better idea than doing what you're supposed to be doing. Most people find it very difficult to be honest with themselves about their ability to put off work. If you are all about deadlines, stress and time management, you are probably not going to think about what you are really doing. If you realize you are procrastinating and you start thinking about it, you have a better chance to take steps to get on with being productive.

Part of avoiding procrastination is to have realistic and achievable goals, ones that are small enough and manageable enough that you don't feel you need to climb Mt. Everest to get the job done. Procrastination is about feeling overwhelmed – either because you find the task to be unpleasant and don't want to experience it or because you are afraid it is too much and you cannot get it done. Perfectionists are often procrastinators.

Scheduling and planning can be powerful tools to help you avoid or conquer procrastination. But they are only effective if you use them. If you are overwhelmed because you lack motivation, you can try things like a cost-benefit analysis of doing vs. not doing the task. You also can create rewards for yourself, a personal carrot-and-stick approach. If you are disorganized and lost, you might use to-do lists and urgent sticky notes. Unless you create and stick to time-bound goals and tasks you will not be effective. Most of us have pages and pages of to-do lists that no human being could complete in the time we have given ourselves to get the job done. They are not realistic. So we have big trouble doing the only thing that will help – and that is doing one small thing at a time.

THE ENDLESS TO-DO LIST

When you set yourself up with unrealistic expectations, it is easier to justify procrastinating. After all, no matter how hard you try, you can't get those six pages of items on your to-do list done today anyway. Setting yourself up to fail is linked to protectionism, self-doubt, shame, guilt and fear. The more unrealistic you make it, the easier it is to say f---it. This is where the idea behind so many time management techniques is derived. Break it down, prioritize and let yourself feel good about what you have accomplished.

In order to overcome the endless to-do list, you must be willing to look at the demands you are placing on yourself and what your priorities are. Then comes being authentically productive so you can create the work-life balance you said you wanted. If you are always avoiding a task, ask yourself why you are avoiding it. What is the future reward? What is your biggest fear? What do you expect to gain or lose by getting it done or not getting it done?

If it seems overwhelming, break it down and make it more manageable. The old adage of taking baby steps holds true. To be authentically productive, you have to do something and you have to do something that is related to achieving your priorities. You need more than just inspiration and creativity. You need to take action to be productive. It can be thought action or doing action. Authentic productivity means moving toward what you want to accomplish.

You are probably not always going to be comfortable while working to be authentically productive. Once you have mastered the art of acting with autonomy and setting and enacting your own priorities, you then must put the pedal to the metal and get things done. You are being authentically productive if you are accomplishing what you want to and you feel good about it. If you feel guilty, weak, ashamed, anxious or overly stressed, you don't need to complete complicated calendars or add more to your already exhaustive to-do list. You need to get to it and do it. Then sit back and applaud yourself for how well you are doing and let go of the "it-is- never-enough" guilt. As long as you are enacting your priorities and making progress, you are being authentically productive.

THE NEED TO BE RIGHT

Most of us like to be right. We feel much better about things when we feel that our opinion counts and that what we think matters. Unfortunately, being right is not all it is cracked up to be. Doing the right thing might be more important than being right. If we take action and make a mistake at least we are moving toward being authentically productive. If we let inertia overtake us because we want to be right, we go nowhere. The virtual environment is alienating to begin with; couple it with the need to be right all the time and you set yourself up to fail.

Being right has the power to alienate all of those folks who do not think you are right. It is a costly price to pay to keep your ego satisfied. In the virtual world, an ego unchecked can run rampant. It is necessary to be independent but not at the expense of others. This is why collaboration and social networking has become such an integral part of working virtually. The human-to-human connection and the importance of opinions, thoughts and feelings of others are missing unless you are connected.

All our lives, we are taught the importance of being right. In K-12 education and on through most of higher education, the right answer is what is prized. Right is what is rewarded and wrong is what is punished. As a culture, we have moved a little toward accepting diversity and difference, but we still have a long way to go. We readily accept that if there are two or three ways to do something, one has to be the "right" way and superior to the others. We are taught to be narrow-minded, judgmental, moralistic and lack empathy. We are taught to compete and compare and always have the right answer. So we should not be surprised when we grow up and become adults with these characteristics.

In the virtual world, it is even more difficult to justify being right at all costs because the costs are so high. The environment is already isolating and alienating. You really can't make judgments the way you did in a face-to-face world because the cues are different. You don't have body language, three dimensions or the benefit of sensing the person's energy first-hand. In the virtual world, you need to give folks more room. You want to be more open-minded and less critical and you certainly want to give them every indication of validation and connection.

Collaboration has become the buzzword of virtual interactions for a reason, because we are all in this together. Our entire view of life and reality is being altered by the integration of technologies into our lives. As Sherry Turkle wrote in her book *Alone Together*, our emotional risks are higher. Even though we are more connected, we are really more alone. "We may be free to work from anywhere, but we are also prone to being lonely everywhere. In a surprising twist, relentless connection leads to a new solitude. We turn to new technology to fill the void, but as technology ramps up, our emotional lives ramp down (Turkle, 2010)."

Right also tends to stand in the way of being authentically productive. The need to be right will keep you from making those first crucial steps to get things done. To be authentically productive, you need to be accountable for what you do. Results are what matter in the virtual workplace and how you get there is open for you to choose as long as you are within the limits of the law and your own moral code. "Choose to be effective. Choose to be open. Choose to be happy. Being right is overrated (Wakeman, 2013)."

Right is also very relative. Think about the things in your lifetime you were sure were right at one time, but have changed and now we know they are not. You don't have to go back to "The world is flat" or "Letting out a little blood will fix you right up" to know that right is a moving target. The real issue is that it is moving faster and faster. It is much more difficult to tell what is right in a detached virtual environment. It is also why we hang on to the illusion of right even more vehemently. It is so easy to blame the team, the boss or the organization: Your client should have been so-and-so. The company is always doing such-and-such; they really must do it my way! The team is really disorganized; they should get it together so I can do my job. You get the idea – should, must, never and always are words that are absolutes, which make you right and the rest of the universe wrong. These attempts at being right rob you of the flexibility, agility and responsiveness necessary to be authentically productive in the virtual workplace.

POSSIBILITIES AND LIMITATIONS

Focusing on limitations will keep you where you are; focusing on possibilities will get you going. If you Google search "limitations" and "possibilities," about six million results will show up. Obviously, they have meaning to a lot of people. From medicine to GPS to teacher education, people are interested in possibilities and limitations. Working in the virtual world is no different. It is a world of opposites, dichotomies and contradictions. It is work without the physical location or place we called "work." It is geographically detached yet virtually connected. It is: open and flexible, but grounded on a common business vision; vulnerable to change, but highly adaptable; private on a personal level, but demands collaboration across boundaries; highly informal, but results-oriented. All of these were discussed in Chapter 1, but it is worth mentioning them again because it is these contrasts that may make being authentically productive seem challenging.

When you are geographically detached yet virtually connected, you have to reach out and rely on people in a different way than you did in the old office. You want to be more considerate of where they are, what time it is, what you are asking for and when you expect it. Avoid sarcasm and inappropriate humor. Be aware that what you are saying and how it is being interpreted might be different. You are responsible for establishing and maintaining trust in these relationships. It takes time to establish trust online and it can be gone in an instant.

You want to be part of the solution, not part of the problem. Your company, school or client needs your buy-in and you want to feel comfortable with the goals, objectives and mission statement you are buying into. It is this common business vision that unites an otherwise chaotic world. It defines the important things and supports productivity. Flexible doesn't mean scattered all over the place. It is possible to be flexible and focused at the same time. Flexibility and focus will help you adapt to, and be productive in, a world that is constantly shifting and changing.

This endless environment of change requires workers who are open to the new. These new technologies are vulnerable to change but highly adaptable. We are continuously adapting them to do more for us in myriad different ways. When the head of HR at Yahoo said, "Speed and quality are often sacrificed when we work from home," and "We need to be one Yahoo! And that means being physically together," it proved yet again that even those in the business struggle with handling the rate of change technology is imposing (Thompson, 2013). We are all vulnerable to change, and change is not something most companies, organizations or people handle really well. Yet in this ever-evolving and morphing workplace, change is a constant.

This environment provides some personal privacy and the illusion of much more. Yet to be both productive and creative, you need collaboration. "Telework makes you more productive and working together makes you more creative" (Thompson, 2013). Working across boundaries means more than just physical boundaries. These boundaries include cultures, race, ethnicity, physical location, gender, generations, time zones and maybe even oceans! Our greatest limitations are our thoughts, not where we are. Serendipity online happens in a different way.

It is not the spontaneous water cooler that is important; it is a connection of minds. A great deal of research shows that virtual workers are more productive and get more done. Just like possibilities and limitations, much of what goes on in the virtual work environment appears to be opposites. Some folks believe that productivity and creativity are opposites, but not in the virtual environment. If you are authentically productive in the virtual environment you are also highly creative and creatively productive. You have to be. In the knowledge economy, "thinking work" is the mainstay. Observation is an obsolete way of determining if workers are really productive.

This new environment and the virtual workers in it are also highly informal but results-oriented. If you can work in your pajamas and get results, that is what is important – results. This requires the company to define exactly what is expected and what success looks like. Yet few companies are currently capable of doing this. Evolving from an era of management by observation, vague goals and less real leadership, many companies are struggling with setting clear expectations. Performance reviews and systems will only be as helpful as they are useful. Informal means being without pretense and formality, not conforming to prescribed regulation and rules, being relaxed and casual. To too many companies, organizations and institutions, it also means less control, a concept that causes fear. Without a clear definition of success, it is difficult to know if you hit the target.

CREATIVITY, CURIOSITY, AND INQUISITIVENESS

You are by nature a curious creature. You are born ready to learn; from that point forward, you are curious, unless someone or some situation trains it out of you. We want to "know" and we are always interested in something new. Esteemed psychologist Lev Vygotsky said learning is a social activity. He was not alone. We have pretty much adapted the philosophy that we do not learn as much or as well when we are alone. It is the interactions, particularly the human interactions, which help us learn new things.

There is a reason that innovation is the number-one attribute every business in the 21st century is embracing. "Innovate or die" seems to be the mantra. "We need leaders who are innovators!" cry the thinkers in business and education. To innovate means to do something new. Yet in most of these areas, we spend a great deal of effort trying to cling to something old. We vehemently deny the new and try to turn back time. Innovation requires us to look forward. Looking forward starts with accepting where we are and then planning to do something new. Innovation in business is difficult because "strategy is about achieving objectives, while innovation is about discovery, we never know exactly where we're going until we get there" (Satell, 2013). Authentic productivity in the virtual workplace requires both strategy and innovation. It requires management to step up the competence, commitment and clarity to innovate. It also requires them to put resources behind their words.

Creativity, curiosity, and inquisitiveness are attributes to be rewarded in the virtual workplace. Innovation in business is dependent on fostering these tendencies. This means that both management and individuals want to position themselves so they feel safe, less stressed and less fearful. Fear and stress are creativity killers. Curiosity is about looking at possibilities not limitations. Inquisitiveness is the willingness to step out on the limb and take a chance and to look at problems in a different light, to look at what is in a new way. Inquisitiveness asks, "Why?" Curiosity asks, "Why not?" And Creativity asks, "How?" In order to be authentically productive working virtually, all three are important. The more you are engaged with what you do, the easier it is to enjoy and value your work. You are much more likely to be authentically productive when you feel that what you do matters.

Meet Michelle

Michelle had never taught online before but she was willing to give it a try. She graduated from the University of Arizona and had spent a lot of time in corporate training but had never taught online. When she taught her first class, she jumped right in. She was a natural. With very little instruction on what to do, she communicated with her students and ran her class with ease. She was organized, got the information out to people, met with learners on a regular basis and never made excuses. She showed up and everything ran smoothly. She even went to Starbucks when the electricity went out during Hurricane Sandy and class went on. If she had any issues, she asked. Approachable and organized, she made a great online teacher. Her learners loved her, she got great class evaluations and her learners learned to apply design principles and create good visuals. What characteristics and behaviors do you think helped Michelle adjust to this environment and be so productive?

Meet Carol

Carol was an experienced teacher with a good background in technology when she came to work for me. She should have made a great online teacher but she always struggled. She had a mother who was elderly and ill. Her computer broke down or had issues at least every other week. She had a hard drive crash or two, a laptop malfunction, and files disappeared. She had a good amount of experience in online learning, but the technologies were always causing her problems. Classes got cancelled, learners complained and there was not much positive communication going on. Carol also worried a lot about everything: her mother, her learners, and her performance. She also had a son who was going through a difficult divorce. There were so many excuses; all seemed to be legitimate, but they were never-ending. If it wasn't one thing that did not work for Carol, it was something else. She had to miss class because she had to take her mother to the doctor's. She couldn't get the papers graded on time because her laptop had problems. She wanted to reach out and call one of the learners, but her son was in town and she needed to talk to him – after all, he was getting a divorce. Her health wasn't too great, either. She always had something: a cold, a sore throat, a stomach problem. Carol is always busy; in fact, she is usually overwhelmed. What might be going on here? What advice would you offer Carol on being authentically productive?

Respond-Ability Exercises: Be Authentically Productive

Exercise 1: What keeps you from getting it done?

Please select all that apply to you:

I am all over the place. I like too many things.

I don't really want to do this. I really want to be a _____ (doctor, lawyer, programmer, or counselor, chef...whatever).

I never have enough time. I am time-poor.

I never have trouble starting things, but I don't finish them.

I am OK once I get going. It is getting started that is hard.

I keep changing my mind.

I just get too frustrated and give up.

I am always starting something new, but I never stick with it.

I start to feel guilty when I am doing really well, and I stop.

Exercise 2: Seven-, 14-, 28-, 56-, 112-Day Commitment

Go back to the list of Rocking Chair goals (pg. 133). Pick one item from the six-month list to make a seven-day list. Commit to focusing on it and doing something about it for seven days. Now select another item from the one-year, five-year and 10-year Rocking Chair Goals lists. Commit to focusing on and taking at least one action each day towards achieving them for 14, 28, 56 and 112 days. Write them down in a journal. On a daily basis, reflect on what you did and how you're doing at focusing on, and achieving, your goals.

Exercise 3: Slow down to get more done.

You need time to be authentically productive. Many people are very busy but marginally productive. If you are moving too fast, chances are you will either burn out or you're missing something somewhere. The only way to identify why is to slow down. Pick something interesting to learn and commit to it for the next three months. The only rule is it has to be something different than what you do now and it has to be interesting to you. It does not have to be job-related or useful. Spend a minimum of two hours a week on learning something new.

Exercise 4: Excuses and Dreams

Excuses and alibis are just a way of saving face. You fall back on these when you are worried about what others think of you and you want to look good in their eyes. This is normal, natural and human. The real problems begin when you start making excuses to yourself and sacrifice what you want because you start to believe your own lies. Make no mistake about it: excuses are lies or half-truths.

The real question is, why are you doing this? How can you recognize the pattern of behavior and stop it?

Take a piece of paper and draw five columns on it. In Column 1, write 25 things you will do this week (put down more if you are motivated). In Column 2 and, write, "Have to" and "Want to." Put an H or a W in the column for each item you wrote down.

How many "Have to's" do you have? How many "Want to's"? It is rare to make up an excuse about something you really want to do!

Exercise 5: Emotional Risk

Now, in Columns 3, 4 and 5 respectively write, "Family expects it," "Society expects it," "Work expects it." Put a check in Columns 3, 4 or 5 by each "Have to" from Exercise 4. Now comes the fun part. You get to ask yourself, "Why?" Why do you think you "have to" do these things and, most importantly, why don't you want to? Take a close look at this one. It is a key to the resistance you feel and why you think you have to make up excuses and alibis. Are you doing these things because you are afraid you will not please somebody? Do you feel a duty or sense of guilt about responsibilities to family, work or society?

Now, if you want to, go back and rewrite the list.

Exercise 6: Virtual Success Groups

Everybody needs somebody and that is true in the virtual environment as well. Your life will be better if you have competent people around you to support you and help you through the ups and downs. You can form a virtual success team. No family and no co-workers permitted on this team. Just pick five or six friends or comfortable acquaintances and form a support group. Give yourselves a name and meet regularly: weekly, bimonthly or monthly.

7

Make Responsible Choices

"You can pretend to care, but you can't pretend to show up."

-- George L. Bell

In order to make responsible choices, first you have to accept responsibility for your thoughts and actions. Your mind and emotions will play tricks on you, if you are not aware. "The buck stops here" was popularized by President Harry S. Truman, who kept a sign with that phrase on his desk in the Oval Office. There are lots of ways this old saying can be interpreted, but generally it means, "I accept responsibility." Behind many of our excuses is the belief that we are not in control. As human beings, we have developed coping mechanisms to give ourselves a sense of control whether it is really true or not.

The closer and more attached we are to others, the more we can allow ourselves to be influenced by their behaviors. It doesn't matter who it is – boss, mom or the kids – the closer we are to someone emotionally, the more we have a tendency to react and not respond to their actions.

People flip our switches, pull our chains and push our buttons. With personality traits tagged passive, aggressive, and passive-aggressive, we allow ourselves to fall victim to the sway of others. "Passive" describes a detached individual, one who is not involved or not showing visible reactions to circumstances or events that might evoke emotions or active participation. Passive people influence us by not being there for us. They are not holding up their share of the bargain, not carrying their weight on the project, not getting involved. The inference is that these people are acted upon rather than causing action. Active is the opposite of passive. Passive people are seen as not being at fault when things go wrong; after all, they didn't do anything.

In some ways, "aggressive" is easier to detect. These people are angry and forceful. They yell, scream and maybe bully. They take action and that action may be outwardly directed or inwardly directed. It can be healthy and constructive or unhealthy and destructive. Aggressive people act; in fact, they may attack.

"Passive-aggressive" is another interesting way humans attempt to control others and cover their motives at the same time. Passive-aggressive behaviors can be manipulative and are almost always negative. Such people are usually trying to gain some kind of control because they are angry but not able to express their anger. This personality trait can be difficult to detect and very destructive to work and personal relationships over time. Passive-aggressive people break down trust. Their behavior is based on the premise that, "I can control you and you can't touch me." This is a very destructive pattern because it is not only difficult to detect but also often self-sabotaging. Here are some ways it might surface: silence when there are issues to discuss, avoiding/ignoring, burying the head in the sand, stonewalling, procrastinating, deliberately stalling, fearing or avoiding competition, ambiguity, sulking, being morose, sullen or resentful in order to get attention or sympathy, chronic lateness or forgetting, fear of intimacy, taking the role of victim, self-pity, blame and making excuses (Harrn, 2011).

There are many ways this kind of behavior can show up. Most of us have some signs of passive, aggressive or passive-aggressive behaviors occasionally. If you or your loved ones are prone to occasionally acting poorly, be aware that what is important is how you respond to others and their actions because you can do nothing to control them. What you can do is control yourself and how you respond to people. You need to learn to be assertive and change the relationships you have with others. You might even want to change the relationship you have with yourself. Psychologists may possibly tell you to set some boundaries.

As discussed earlier, in the virtual world you are often alone with yourself. This has been stated before but it cannot be over-emphasized. You may be connected instantaneously to friends, family and the world but, as Sherry Turkle put it, we are "alone together" (Turkle, 2012).

The idea of self as the totality of your thoughts and feelings is not new. The concept of "self" is based on your physicality, thoughts and feelings. When you reference "self," you refer to yourself as an object. The concept of self has major implications for the individual's behaviors and interactions with others. Even after a half-century of psychological research and debate, the concept of self is still mysterious. Most people would agree, though, that it starts with a sense of self-awareness.

As far as we know, only the human species is self-consciousness. Humans can stand outside of themselves and judge, condemn, feel pride, shame or guilt, and describe themselves. Many psychologists have tried to put a label on exactly what this thing called "self" is: Freud's ego (1951), Horneys's real self (1950), Maslow's self-actualized person (1954), and Mead's "I" (1934) are only a few examples. This self-concept is the picture we have of ourselves and is not necessarily related to reality.

What is interesting in the virtual environment is our ability to redefine this picture, to go beyond the limits (good and not-so-good) that we would have as individuals in the face-to-face world. We have a tendency to de-individuate and construct different versions of the way we see ourselves, the way we would like to see ourselves, and the way we

166

present ourselves to others. This constructing and reconstructing of our self through interaction has led to an explosion of socially networked online connections. This is how we establish our social identities.

Identity takes form from the time we are infants. It is developed by the human cognitive characteristic of categorizing and pigeonholing. We are male or female, Indian or Italian, Jewish or Catholic, doctor or lawyer, Democrat or Republican. We are either in the friends group on Facebook or one of the contacts on LinkedIn. We use group labels to define who we are. We also use individual labels like names. Online, we get to be creative with those labels. We can change from Joe Smith to BananaJoe and create an entirely new online identity. Our sense of personal worth can be contingent upon this identity. Identity can be related to the prestige of the labels used to create it. How people respond is often affected by their social identity.

Social identity also gives us archetypes and role models. Since consciousness has to be present in order to have self-consciousness, this image of who we are as individuals evolves gradually out of social experiences. Our experiences online with social relationships – and even how we interact and relate – is distorted through a veil of technologies. We see ourselves totally differently than we really are and that is not only OK, but often accepted and encouraged. We join groups and get involved in massive online games to become someone else. Online lets us adapt our self to new and virtual worlds. It may not matter if you are the Guardian Fighter trying to fix The Holy Trinity at the local gas station but it is important in MMORPG (massive multiplayer online role playing game) space.

All of this is enormously complex but it comes down to this: online you have more choices and also more responsibility for how you define yourself. It is not a simple case of the parts adding up to the whole. The concept of self is a complex synthesis of every conscious moment, our environment, interactions, thoughts, feelings and the individual's perceptual field. It is all remarkably diverse and reflects the attitudes you have toward something. These attitudes often determine how we respond. They can differ in content, direction, intensity, clarity, consistency, salience and accuracy (Rosenburg, 1986). Responding in an environment where many boundaries are no long present makes responding with intent even more challenging. When working online, one of the first areas of challenge you will notice is in personal boundaries.

PERSONAL BOUNDARIES: TIME, SPACE, EMOTIONAL, PHYSICAL, RELATIONSHIP AND SOCIAL

Have you ever felt at a loss when you didn't get done what you wanted to get done and the week is over? Have you put yourself at a disadvantage when you failed to tell someone, "No"? Have you ever felt manipulated or mistreated when someone kept you from doing what you needed to because they knew how to push your buttons? Virtual workers have to learn to set their own boundaries, for a lot of reasons.

Boundaries are less well-defined in the virtual world and this can be challenging for many of us.

It is critical that you learn to set time boundaries because the online world is nonstop. It never turns off. It never takes a day of vacation. It is always on. "I love my devices and services, I love being connected to the global hive mind…but I am more aware of the price we pay: lack of depth, reduced accuracy, lower quality, impatience, selfishness, and mental exhaustion to name but a few" (Thurston, 2013).

Many of us have felt a disconnection even while being connected. Stress develops from a schedule that has us constantly connected and is enhanced by our addiction to constant connectivity. We lose time, patience and even our sense of humor because we are always on. We feel obligated to be there even when on vacation. We feel obligated to return the email right away. We feel obligated to respond to the pokes, the messages, the voice mails and all the other things that are coming at us constantly. Time boundaries are about choosing when, and to what, we will respond or not respond.

Perhaps you have had the experience of walking into a restaurant, seeing a gorgeous young couple on a date and witnessing both of them talking on their cell phones, totally engaged and paying no attention to each other. Many of us have developed these outrageous and ridiculous behaviors; we take our email (not our significant other) to bed with us. We sit down in the family room to watch television and wind up posting on a social network all night. If you are feeling like you are always on, never relaxed and guilty because you didn't respond quickly enough, you might want to set some time boundaries.

Space was a boundary in the physical world that was an absolute. You ate in the dining room, slept in the bedroom and worked in the office. The limits and behaviors coincided. They matched up. But with the breaking down of walls and limits, these have become blurred. More than anything else, space boundaries provide us with a sense of order. We have national boundaries, state boundaries and local boundaries. Personal space boundaries are no different. Even the cubicle had us within our own space, with limits. In the virtual environment, it is important to put some of these boundaries back into place. Set up a workplace for work. And you might want to stop checking email in the smallest room in the house.

Boundaries are so important that the founding fathers established the Fourth Amendment to the Constitution to address the issue. They thought that happiness could not be achieved without "The right of the people to be secure…with their persons…houses…papers and effects…shall not be violated." Some people will lump physical boundaries and space, but physical boundaries really are your things and stuff, too. This can mean your online space and computer space as well. This is a topic of hot controversy and about to get hotter. Globally, we are experiencing "Big Data." We download and sign on to apps and, in many cases, give away a lot of our physical boundaries without even knowing it. Under the illusion of "free" use, we have given technologies access to our personal lives. Physical boundaries are important because they delineate our sense of privacy.

These boundaries let you know when your privacy is being violated. By working at home in your pajamas, you are in some ways already breaking old boundaries. Pajamas were for sleeping and privacy. Home was for family and friends; now it is an office. You don't want people going through your purse or hacking your website either because that is a violation of your physical boundaries. Whether it is your desk drawers, your email or your body, physical boundaries are both personal and private "things" that belong to you. If you are feeling violated, exposed or watched, you might want to think about setting some physical boundaries.

You need to set up some relationship boundaries to maintain healthy relationships. Healthy relationships allow you to function freely and with positive self-regard. Both virtual and face-to- face relationships are healthier if the boundaries provide clarity. To establish boundaries, you must be clear about what you want and what you don't want. Fear is one of the biggest influences on relationship boundaries. If you are concerned about being popular, liked, loved or just a people pleaser, you might want to think about setting some relationship boundaries.

Emotional boundaries are a little more complicated. When you are at work, you think and act professionally. Why? Because you are a professional and you are at work. The overarching expectation for most work situations is that you act with the best interests of the company in mind and conduct all business accordingly. So you are cold, calculating and on task. Your behaviors are confined to what is appropriate and limited to those people who are part of your business circle. Lovers, family and friends are not part of this environment, so they are not included in how you act at work. These are outside of the scope of work; emotional behaviors are off-limits. You leave your private life at the door and bring only your professional persona into play.

This persona is your business identity or your façade. It is the mask you wear while you do the job. Some people's business persona is much nicer than their private persona, while others hide private secrets behind their mask. You can't always tell who is the gambler, the domestic violence victim, the lonely divorcee, the estranged father, or the financially strapped person. Virtual workers are constantly reminded of their situations because the mask is off.

Emotional boundaries are tough, especially with our inner circle. Emotional boundaries are about letting other people push our buttons. How much are you willing to give? How much do you want to be in control of what you feel? Setting emotional boundaries helps us establish healthy relationships and avoid unhealthy, dysfunctional relationships. Unhealthy emotional boundaries cause emotional pain, blame and resentment. When you have weak emotional boundaries, you are greatly affected by others' words, thoughts, and actions. Weak emotional boundaries will cause you to blame others and give up responsibility for your own feelings. This is often a result of not being taught good healthy emotional boundaries as a child. Nevertheless, emotional boundaries are important when you are at work in the virtual world. You need to be able to say, "No." Healthy emotional boundaries allow you to follow your own priorities, pursue your own goals and take responsibility for yourself. If you are feeling like a victim, a martyr or a scapegoat you might want to set some emotional boundaries.

We are afraid we will not be liked, accepted, admired, or perfect. We try to be too many things to other people and we forget the most important relationship we have, the one with our self. The more intimate a relationship, the more difficult it is to draw these boundaries. When we don't establish these relationship boundaries with our clients, bosses, colleagues or family and friends, we put these relationships in jeopardy

Challenging social boundaries in the virtual environment helps to open up opportunities and create insights. We are always being socialized. From the time we are children until the day we die we are subtly being told to fit in. Not surprisingly, social network connectivity has both highlighted and contributed to challenging the validity of many of these boundaries. Professions, communities of practice, online identities and traditional sex, gender, class, culture, ethnic and racial boundaries are being challenged. Appropriate behaviors and norms are being blown away as boundaries break down across contexts and groups. Social and collective identity has been redefined to include virtual environments. Social boundaries, especially online, are crossed constantly.

Social boundaries, however, are more than the big picture. These extend to the way we act and what is socially appropriate to do in a particular social context. Individuals use many of these to include or exclude themselves or others from particular groups. Taken to extremes, these social boundaries help us define what is real. They influence our thoughts and behaviors to such an extent that we come to believe they are facts. Interestingly, the virtual environment has its own very different set of social boundaries. Stalking, creeping, phishing and adapting are all words that have different meanings online. Social boundaries online and off are changing rapidly and being challenged by a crowdsourcing world that is rewriting what is real and what is acceptable.

Many people communicate online in order to get a reaction. They post outrageous comments, send inappropriate emails, or upload immature videos. They act in ways that demonstrate a lack of social boundaries. This is compounded by an online world that stores and manipulates data for sensation. Reputations can be ruined, lives destroyed and hearts broken because someone posted or shared something that is totally inappropriate. If you have ever felt bullied, picked on or like an outcast, you might want to consider setting some social boundaries.

SETTING BOUNDARIES

Setting boundaries is one of the most important parts of success in relationships. This is true of our relationships with time, space, emotions, physical conditions and human relationships. To function well, we have to set boundaries that work for us. We all have had experience with poor boundaries, boundaries that are too loose or too strict, boundaries that are not working. So how do you change this?

The first step in setting boundaries is to get in touch with you. Ask yourself what will make you comfortable? If the problem is a physical boundary, you may need to close the door, lock the door or pull the curtain. If that doesn't work, you may need to go to a different physical location. Get out of the house. Rent a space from a work share group or go to the library or Starbucks. What's important is that you identify what you need to accomplish, set your priorities in a realistic fashion and then set up the mechanism to achieve it. Make responsible choices based on your priorities. Being clear about your priorities helps you recognize good compromises. Your priorities are essential to your boundary strategy. If the boundary is an emotional one, you might ask yourself, "How much am I willing to give?" Once you decide what you want and don't want, communicate that to people and keep them informed. You have the choice to be constructive toward boundaries, not destructive.

Some things may be negotiable and some things will not. Scheduling is an example of something that can be either negotiable or nonnegotiable; it depends on you. Perhaps your daughter wants you to drive her to the mall and you had other plans. You negotiate that you will take her and her friend but not until after you finish what you are working on. Nonnegotiable may be the $50 she tries to extract from you because she wants mall money. Scheduling issues can be nonnegotiable too. "I will work 9 a.m. to 4 p.m., Monday through Thursday, but on Friday, I have to leave by 2 p.m. to pick up my children for swim team." When setting boundaries, ask yourself: "Where can I be flexible? And where do I need to hold my ground?"

The most important part of making these choices is asking: Are they working for you? Are you accomplishing what you want? Are you enacting your priorities so that you can meet your goals? There is nothing wrong with making sacrifices, but if you are doing it too frequently, you will wind up feeling resentful.

Technologies can give you the illusion that you are superhuman. There are only 24 hours in a day and you are only one human being. You have limits in terms of your values, time and energy and your desire and ability to sacrifice. These are important issues to understand.

Boundaries are always more difficult to understand when they involve a public stage and private information. Whether it is emails at work or posting on a social website, making responsible choices involves looking at the future of a relationship. What happens if I get fired? Leave for another job? Decide to end this relationship? Start a new one with another person?

Relationship boundaries are probably the most difficult to master from many reasons. They may involve a boss who is challenging, a passive spouse, difficult parents or an unruly child. It helps to identify the issues and situations, and make a plan. Put some thought into what really works for you. Do not expect others to know what you need in relationship boundaries. They are not fortune-tellers and they are not mind readers. Neither are you. You can only identify your side of the boundary.

Making responsible choices requires that you hold up your end. When you set boundaries, stick with them and follow through. If you make commitments in an indulgent moment when your time will not really allow it, you may have to neglect a more important priority. Making responsible choices is not just about taking a specific action or making a particular decision. It is about being responsible to you, being efficient in your choices, connections and self-management.

Sometimes we do not see boundary issues as what they really are because we are trying to people-please, or we want to be wanted. If you take on a problem that belongs to someone else, you have made their problems more important than your own priorities. That will get you into trouble. If someone is making decisions for you, has expectations you do not agree with, takes your stuff, demands your time or is constantly complaining, it is time to look at yourself. This is probably a boundary issue.

Your sense of self and social identity can make it difficult to say "no" to people. If you feel inferior or are worried about approval, fear consequences and feel manipulated, you might want to re-evaluate your choices. Who are you making more important than you? There are old sayings that remain popular for a reason: "Good fences make good neighbors" and "Do not mix business with pleasure" have some truth to them. Boundaries and responsible choices help you keep your limits in check. Not all relationships have the same impact on you. Not all significant others have the same significance. The more significant they are to you, the more they can influence your self-concepts.

Strong boundaries are good for everyone and they are essential to survival working in the virtual environment. *The Pajama Effect* makes you more open, less protected and more vulnerable to boundary disputes. The safety you felt when you had the corner office with the windows and the brass name tag mounted on the door doesn't exist in the virtual world. You are more out in the open, available and vulnerable. Setting boundaries requires a positive and constructive frame of mind. It also helps to have a sense of humor and to be creative. You can mix business and pleasure, but cautiously. It all starts with defining what you want and where you are going to set limits. You want to be focused on how you are making the choices you need to make in order to achieve your priorities.

In the virtual environment, it means you also need to be aware of what is going on with you. This starts with being aware of your thoughts. What are you thinking about all day long? Your conscious mind is within you control. You can control your thoughts but not if you are on autopilot. To make responsible choices, be aware of what you are choosing.

SYMBOLS AND THE SUBCONSCIOUS MIND

The subconscious mind doesn't argue, it doesn't reason and it doesn't analyze. There is a great deal of controversy about the subconscious mind. There are many different definitions and many viewpoints. Psychologists like Carl Jung discussed its importance and relationship to behaviors and the conscious mind. There are many words used to describe "the thing" that makes the hair on your neck stand up and the cut on your finger heal -- none of which are that important to us. Call this "thing" whatever you want to, but understand it is the part of your mind that does deductively what you think about all day long.

In deductive reasoning, a conclusion is reached from general truths; in inductive reasoning, the conclusion is reached from specific examples. Deductive is big to small and inductive is small to big. The truth depends on the premise and that premise can be absurd or true. It does matter. Here is an example: All dogs are animals and this is a dog, then this is an animal. All cats are great hunters and this is a cat, then this is a great hunter. Whoever made the last statement never knew my cat, Buttercup, who managed somehow to miss out on the hunting gene. In deductive reasoning, the conclusion is logically clear even though the premise is absurd. Inductive reason builds on events to draw a conclusion in the future. Here is an example of inductive reasoning: All the people I know carry their phones with them all day and all night; therefore, everyone carries their phones with them at all times. The important thing about deductive reasoning and the subconscious mind is its ability to bring about a result.

The subconscious works on suggestion. It doesn't analyze whether the suggestion is true or false, it just proceeds to do what it does. Joseph Murphy popularized the subconscious mind and ushered in the mind-body connection in 1963 when he wrote, "As a man thinks, feels and believes, so is the condition of his mind, body and circumstances" (Murphy, 1963). Advertisers and companies know this and are experts at using it to get you to buy things. Politicians and governments know this and are experts at using it to get you to support causes. The thing believed in does not matter, it is the thought or symbol that does.

The seeds have been planted. We buy pills because they have been represented to us by commercials showing better lifestyles. We see the elephant and the donkey and thoughts of political differences bubble up and we react. The thoughts are flowing from patterns that have been established by us through a lifetime of living. Symbols are established through our use of the senses and then recalled when something cues them in our mind. When you see the symbol "©" you know it means the copyright. When you see "☺" you know it is the smiley face. When you hear a siren, you know it means the police or firefighters are close. When you smell cinnamon, it means the holiday season is here. Through the ages, many artists, writers, singers and inventors have known that suggestion is a powerful tool.

You have been conditioned to think of work as a place, so establish one. When you are in this space you will more likely be able to keep your thoughts on work because you have established it as your workplace. You are not here to do laundry or shop. You are here to work. What kinds of simple suggestions might you want to send to yourself when you are working in the virtual environment? Start with a simple symbol, like the company logo on your screen saver or your mouse pad. You might want to add a picture of the virtual team on the desktop or a calendar. When you are in your workspace, place things nearby to remind yourself that you are working. Simple symbols and suggestions like this help more than you would imagine.

The next step might be to get out of your pajamas and put on a work outfit. If you dress for work, you are more likely to do work. You certainly don't have to wear a suit every day, but it would not hurt, either. Wear a casual outfit if that fits your style and personality, but be sure you are sending a signal that when you are in these clothes you are at work. Get out of the exercise clothes and the lounge apparel: it is too personal, too relaxed and you are sending the wrong signal if you want to get work done.

Your subconscious mind cannot argue with you and you cannot argue with it. That is the job of consciousness to dispute, focus and pay attention. Your subconscious mind is the seat of habit. It is very powerful, much more powerful than conscious attention. Your subconscious can help or hurt you when it comes to getting things done. The habits you form in thought and beliefs establish patterns in your subconscious mind. Make sure that the thoughts are ones that allow you to achieve the outcomes you really want. Your subconscious mind reacts, your conscious mind responds. Your conscious mind is capable of thinking things out for itself. Your subconscious reacts to symbols and has no preference for one course of action over another.

Be aware of your thought habits. Become aware of what you think about all day long. Suggestion is the mental process of putting something into your mind, either a thought or an idea. Then you have the choice consciously of entertaining it, accepting it, putting it into action or disputing it. But you can only do this if you are aware. Your conscious mind has the power to recognize suggestions and reject them. A suggestion has no power over you unless you accept it mentally.

Symbols act like autosuggestions. You can use autosuggestions to overcome fears and responsibly enact your priorities. One technique is to sit quietly, still your mind by breathing or repeating a saying and focusing on what you want. Be positive: "I am working and meeting my goals. I take it one task at a time and I am making progress. I stay on task and do what I need to do. I am responsible and meeting my deadlines." Those little words you say to yourself are very important. What you tell yourself all day is what happens.

The power of suggestion and symbols can be constructive or destructive. You can receive suggestions from other people as well as objects. What is important is that you use suggestions so that you can be successful working in the virtual environment. If you let others rule you through the power of suggestion, you will not be able to achieve the results you want. You will not be able to act with autonomy, set and enact those priorities, be really productive or make responsible choices because you will not be in charge of you. When you turn your power over to symbols and suggestions that do not align with what you want, you pay a price.

Focus on what you want, not what you don't want. Use symbols and suggestions consciously to cue your mind to counteract destructive ideas and unproductive urges. Don't let friends, family, parents, professional associates, or anybody else control your consciousness. It is yours and yours alone. Most negative suggestions are constructed around fear and control. Be in charge of you; let others worry about themselves. You can't think for them and they can't think for you. Think responsibly and you will make responsible choices.

FUN, FROLIC AND FOCUS

Focused consciousness or thought is attention. What you give your attention to, multiplies. And you have a choice, each and every minute, about what you focus on. You cannot erase a negative but you can right now focus on a positive, productive, responsible thought. That is your choice. You have the power to choose. Choose fun, choose frolic and choose success. If you hate what you are doing, it is going to be hard to make yourself do it. If you enjoy it and have a reasonable amount of fun, it makes it so much easier. If you tell yourself, "I just can't get anything done. I can't focus. I am behind and it is hopeless. I better make up an excuse because I will never get this done. This is boring and I can do something else, no one will know," you are setting yourself up for failure. Don't be surprised when it happens. If, on the other hand, you focus on being productive, responsible and having a sense of humor, the virtual environment will be much easier to navigate.

Misunderstandings are common in an environment with so many cues missing. Do not take it personally. When in doubt, ask. The folks on the other end of the technology are new to this also. They are as confused as you are on how to stay focused and be happy. Choose to give them the benefit of the doubt. When you read that email or text, remember it is not meant to be a personal negative directed toward you. You are the one choosing to take it that way.

Ask yourself, "Is this rational? Is it even true? What am I reading into this? How am I bringing my thoughts and meaning into this interpretation? Might there be another way to think about this?" And then think about it in another way or think about something else altogether. Get your mind off the topic. Stop running it through your mind like a video stuck in a loop. Get over it and do not take it personally. Making the right decisions allows you to have fun, frolic and play, but stay focused on the tasks you need to complete. Stop creating thoughts of worry, anxiety, excuses and apologies. You can make a decision to act intelligently. Stop underestimating yourself and everybody else.

In *The Pajama Effect* you have more control over your world than ever before. Take advantage of the freedom this atmosphere provides for you, but be aware. The responsibility for your behaviors and your decisions is in your corner. As long as you understand yourself, you will be a highly successful virtual worker. When you take responsibility and stay focused on your priorities you can create a virtual environment that is productive, connected and in your control.

So, stop blaming others and a make a decision right now to be responsible for your choices. Look inside yourself and make decisions that are right for you. Remember the power of the word "no". It is clear and direct and to the point. If you want to eliminate things that are unwanted from your life, start saying "no" and forget about feeling guilty. Make a decision to stay focused on what you want. Indecision is the decision not to decide. When you think independently and act with autonomy you have more freedom, and with more freedom comes more responsibility. In the virtual environment, you cannot abdicate the responsibility to others and expect it to get done. You want to state your expectations – of yourself, your family and your coworkers. The clearer you are about these expectations the happier and more productive you will be. Your expectations are easier to meet if they are clearly expressed.

Meet Kathy

Kathy is new to telecommuting. She works from home three times a week and the other two days she works from the main office. Kathy works for an auto insurance company, providing quotes for corporate vehicle fleets. She dutifully follows the company script and the fee schedule because she is afraid of giving too much flexibility to the client. She does not want to do anything wrong or get in trouble with her boss. One day, however, a very large client asked Kathy to make some urgent changes to their coverage. The changes were nothing out of the ordinary, but she had never dealt with a similar situation. Kathy hesitated, then said she was not able to make a decision and needed to talk to her boss first. Kathy called her boss, but had forgotten that he was out on vacation that week. Unable to get his needs met, the customer called Kathy at the end of the week and switched coverage from her company to one of its competitors. What might Kathy do differently next time? If you were Kathy's supervisor, what would you do to help her?

Meet Mary

Mary likes working from home because she has aging parents and it makes it easier for her to take them to doctors' appointments and do the shopping. Mary is always making excuses for not getting things done on time. But it is not her fault, her parents are demanding and things just seem to happen to her. First, the Internet connection went down, then her computer had a virus, and then her mother fell. Mary loves her job but she is getting deeper and deeper into trouble with her supervisor because she can never meet agreed-upon deadlines. She has her home office in the downstairs den, next to the laundry room. That is a distraction when her laundry has to be done or when her father comes downstairs and stops to chat. What might help Mary be able to meet more deadlines and maybe save her job?

RESPOND-ABILITY EXERCISES: MAKE RESPONSIBLE CHOICES

Exercise 1: Everybody Needs Structure

The key to structure is to keep it simple and make it flexible but definitive. This is especially true in the virtual world because the physical, psychological and emotional boundaries are more open. Make yourself a schedule and write it down. Put it on the wall, if possible, or at least in front of you for a while. On this schedule for the week include projects, processes and personal time, the 3Ps. These 3Ps will help you see where you are out of balance so that you can correct problem areas. Make sure you include the 25 things you came up with in Chapter 6 (Be Authentically Productive), Exercise 5 and more if you want. Take a colored pencil or crayon and color each one in. If you are doing it on a tablet or computer, just highlight the chart in three different colors. What do you see?

Exercise 2: What Choices are You Making?

In the last week did the choices you made lead to any of these:

1.   Rejection

2.   Acceptance

3.   Satisfaction

4.   Enthusiasm

5.   Appreciation

6.   Apprehension

7.   Advancing

8.   Learning

9.   Resentment

10.   Despair

11.   Disappointment

12.   Contentment

What were the events or circumstances that lead you to feel this way? What is the belief you hold? It is always your choice how you feel and or respond to an event. Why did you choose to respond this way? Is it responsible? If you had to do it again would you respond in the same way? How might you change your response?

Exercise 3: Getting the Recognition and Rewards You Deserve

Are you irritable, cynical, critical, defensive or impatient much of the time? Do you have big dreams but no patience with yourself or others? Do you work hard? Do you feel entitled or special? Do you think doing mundane things is beneath you? If you answered "yes" to any of these, ask yourself, "Why?"

Exercise 4: Nothing but the Best

Suppose your boss criticizes you, how does that feel? If you come in second or third or last in something, do you feel less-than? If someone corrects you or gives you negative feedback on your work are you hurt? Write a short paragraph of no more than 150 words on the last time you felt upset because you were not "the winner or the best." Take no more than 10 minutes to do this exercise.

Exercise 5: The Happy Ending

If you could change a situation that you are currently in so that it had a happy ending, what would that look like? How would it be different? What would change? Make a list of specific events. This list can be as long as you want. Take your time and think about what you are expecting.

Now, after each event, put how you achieved this result: Prince Charming, the Fairy Godmother or Hard Work. This exercise is about determining if you are waiting for a miracle or a bolt of lightning to save you from your current situation. If you are, you are probably not going to make responsible choices. If you feel worthy but powerless to affect your life, you have created a situation where you are helpless and a victim. You are trapped. Be realistic, you can't change other people. Focus on what you can do and what you can work on.

Exercise 6: Springing the Trap

Now look at that list again. Next to each item, write one small thing you will do to make the situation different in the next week, six months and in a year. If you write it down, you are responsible for making it happen. Make these attainable and executable by you and you alone.

8

Align Connections

"I believe the choice to be excellent begins with aligning your thoughts and words with the intention to require more from yourself."

-- *Oprah Winfrey*

You can be waiting in line at the grocery store, at your kid's soccer game or almost anywhere and order almost anything. We are no longer pinned to the device; the devices come with us wherever we go. The industrial age created isolated life functions in the same way it created isolated job functions. Fortunately, the virtual environment is helping to put an end to all of that. It is much more natural when we blend work, learning and living. People are, by nature, blended creatures. Information has been available anywhere anytime for the last 15 years, and now has become even more available with mobile access. Higher speeds and better devices allow us to do our banking, shopping, working and learning from almost anywhere.

More sites are going mobile and more people have access to audio, data and multimedia. Information is being aggregated and mobile is replacing .com. You can interact with your mobile devices by touch, voice, location or video. You no longer need to type. The search function has been amended to supply you with exactly what you need when you need it. You can find local restaurants, game scores, bank hours, even local news. You search and you get results. The major search engines understand "big data" about where you are, what you buy, who you buy it from. If you're looking for answers, you can text or search "Eagles Football score from Sunday, October 28" and, voilà! There it is. It doesn't matter if you are in the train, on the plane or at the beach, you can access the office or library, shop for clothes and talk to your friends (Fox, 2008).

BLENDING OF WORK AND PLAY

All of this connection comes with a cost. Interactions used to be more linear. You got up in the morning and the stores were not open yet, so you couldn't shop. You had breakfast and went to work. While you were at work, you worked. You couldn't shop there, so you waited until your lunch hour or after work and then you went to the store. The segments of time and functions of your day aligned your interactions.

People's lives, motivations and identities centered on their surroundings and whether they were at work or not. Things were linear: first you went to school, then you went to work, then you retired. We used to transition in stages, time segments and life phases. Now we move through social experiences and diverse, complicated life involvements, from education to romance, on a device. The boundaries between work and play, student and worker, shopping and dating have blurred significantly.

Certainly, socioeconomic backgrounds, expectations and education figure into your identity. One's identity is developed through a range of influences, practices, relationships and experiences. Identity is being developed now by being connected via technology. Because we can move so quickly between work and play, there is considerable evidence that young people look at the context of work and play differently. Personal relationships, well-being, lifestyle and play influence connections in the virtual environment.

Since the 2008 banking debacle, people all over the globe are less trusting of the establishment. The idea that you go to school, then graduate and get a good job that you keep for life is antiquated. Young people and others want flexibility and they are not sure that education will lead them to a job. They want options. The concept of career is a balancing act rather than an achievement. Who you are connected to makes all the difference; what you know is optional. Having a number of alternatives and the ability to make choices gives you flexibility (Stokes & Wyn, 2007). Flexibility is what allows you to align your connections with your personal goals. If you want to work less and join the new rich, anything is possible. The message is clear. The old constraints and the old rules about work and play no longer apply. The lines between work and play are becoming very blurred and not always by your choice.

DERAILING SUCCESS

There is a difference between balancing work and play, and blending it. There is a fusion going on: we are always at work and we are always at play. We can't get away from either one. Offices are going home and home is now the office. Employers are offering child care at work so you can bring your children and reimbursing virtual workers for child care to get those kids out of the home office.

We can't get away from being connected. We always have our devices with us and we are always "on." Even the commute is a time to talk to colleagues and call clients. In Hong Kong, you get to choose between sections in the restaurants that permit or ban cellphone use, like smoking and non-smoking. Even when you try to get away for a vacation, work comes with you. You used to be safe from work on airplanes but that changed, too. The ability to connect all over the world 24/7 further erodes your personal time. If you have offices in Asia, you are working the 5 p.m. to 11 p.m. shift. If offices are in Europe and you are in the Americas, you might be up at 3 a.m. to conduct business. You are expected to be everywhere all the time.

This has all happened so fast that the average worker feels overwhelmed. Afraid to say "no," many people don't want to tell their employers not to call on the weekend, or after 7 p.m., or in the morning before they get into the office. The expectations of loyalty are not clear. What is reasonable is undefined. How many email accounts are reasonable? When is it reasonable to expect an email response? All of this connectivity has brought up work and life challenges. One is isolation. It sounds ironic that with all this connectivity, one of the most challenging aspects of *The Pajama Effect* is isolation.

But connecting via a device is different than looking your coworker in the eye and going out to lunch together. Workers who are connected via devices are often uncertain about what is expected and this creates additional anxiety. Having more micro-workers, free agents and job changers in the workforce also means fewer close friends at work and less of a sense of belonging. Over the long run, you are less connected and more alone.

Virtual communities help some, but there is a lot of work for employers to do. Employers tend to treat virtual workers as if they do not exist. You are "out of sight, out of mind." Most importantly, they don't always trust you. Employers need to establish a place where virtual workers can connect with each other and the company. It is important for virtual workers to have a face and a place. Productivity is improved when people feel at home and as if they belong to a greater cause (Challenger, 2002).

People want their own identity within the organization and they want to be recognized and appreciated. No one wants to be faceless or nameless or feel out of the mix. Just as you took items from home and family pictures to work in the cubicle, it might be a good idea to equip the home office with a few elements to remind you of work: photos of the team or coworkers, the company logo, etc. Those reminders connect you with your professional identity.

Depending on where you are, people can seem to have too much access and you may feel you have too little control. Other personal and privacy limits are also breaking down. Where you are and what you are doing is being tracked in the cloud. To use a free app, you give away your location or divulge other personal information. Your personal life is not your own. Your parents can connect with you anytime and so can your children. If your parents want to see their sweetie-pie grandchild, you are expected to put your child on the video stream. Being out-of-town on a business trip is not an excuse to miss little Sara's play – you can catch it on your tablet. You have no excuse for not connecting, but it is not always on your terms (Zimmerman, 2010).

On video chat, your employer can see that your office is a mess and you haven't made your bed. On the other hand, you might find yourself checking your kids' text messages, Facebook pages or tweets. Then there are the children who talk to their parents via text 20, 30, 40 or more times a day. When do they have time to develop their own space, make their own decisions or build their own lives? To get on with life, you need to have a sense of your own identity. You can spend so much time connecting with everybody else that you forget the importance of connecting with yourself (Orenstein, 2009).

Connecting with Self and Then Everybody Else

Self-awareness is the key to aligning connections. Until you stop and realize how you are connecting with yourself and then everybody else, you are not listening. Stop and listen to what you are saying to you. If you want your own successes, you have to align your inner connections. What are you saying to yourself? Are you telling yourself you can't get it done? Are you telling yourself it is too much? Are you telling yourself you can do it all? Are you telling yourself there is no use? You will never make the deadline anyway, so why try? Are you telling yourself you can make up an excuse, that your employer or coworkers will never know the car didn't die or your kid wasn't really sick? Excuses, apologies, alibis and regrets are not on the positive side of connecting. They signify defeat and guilt. Connecting with yourself means letting go of guilt and getting in touch with who and where you really are now. It requires honesty and self-reflection, learning and growing, and being willing to change what isn't working.

Connecting with the self is about accepting yourself without judgment or fear. Start by listening to the messages you are sending yourself. To align your connections, you have to connect with you. If you have trouble with this you are going to have more trouble genuinely connecting with others. The connections or lack of connections with you are often what looks like broken connections with others. When you really know what your inner connections are all about, you have control over how you connect to others.

There are also a lot of voices out there in cyberspace and more coming daily. There are a host of sites, media, apps and texts waiting to draw your attention and influence your feelings. Some have commerce in mind, some want personal relationships and some just seem to want to annoy you. If you listen to everything, you run the risk of not paying attention to you. You can't make everyone happy all the time and it is not your job. Being a people-pleaser is not going to work in the virtual environment. You are probably going to feel resentful because you are not getting the support you need. Some support might be there, but if it is, it is usually under the radar. Most companies are only beginning to understand they need to support folks in the virtual workplace.

When you are not paying attention to you, you are not listening to that little voice inside that is trying to guide you. You are not looking out for your best interests. Then you start to feel bad, resentful, fearful, and doubtful. Not much good is going to come from that. Start listening to what you say to yourself. There are hundreds of self-help books on the power of your thoughts and words, but none can help if you are not paying attention to what you are thinking and saying to yourself. In the online environment, there are many ways you can reflect upon where you truly are. Unlike the 20th century traditional workplace, the virtual workplace is highly informal but results-oriented.

COMMUNICATIONS SKILLS IN THE DIGITAL WORKPLACE

When Frank Lloyd Wright unveiled The Johnson Wax building, he set a new standard for the workplace. No more dirty old factories; it was the dawn of the cubicle, with orderly rows and an orderly environment. Work was a formal place and the expectations of the boss were crystal clear. There was a hierarchy of rank, and management was exacting and fastidious (Godin, 2009).

The new workplace is not like that. It is informal and office complexes are closing. It is a simple case of economics. Traditional offices are disappearing because of their own economic weight. The employer no longer has to pay you to commute to a building to sit at a computer screen all day. In fact, they may not have to pay you at all. There is a global workforce and people in India and Botswana who would be happy to have your job for far less pay. Work is being auctioned off to the lowest bidder and that makes for a lot more workplace stress. Everyone and everything can be outsourced, especially if the price is right. Everything is traceable and measurable. After all, it is all-digital. Your employer knows when you are working, exactly what you are working on, with whom you connect, and when you are connected. If it can be measured, it will be measured. As management guru Peter Drucker said, if you want to manage it, you have to measure it.

There is no room for fluff or people who are not essential to the business. Are you an essential employee? You are if you bring in business, manage customers, clients or fans, or keep the virtual community functioning. Along with the talents and skills of designers, engineers, entrepreneurs and technicians, the virtual workplace needs talented communicators. These are people who can bring people together. These are people who can get results in the virtual environment (Capurro & Pingle, 2002).

CULTURAL BARRIERS AND CHALLENGES

Cultural barriers separate us from others. We all know the world is growing smaller and we are more connected to each other. But these connections have to come at a more integral level than through just using technologies; they have to be on an individual, personal and human level. The mental processes and rules of interacting in business and life are strongly influenced by the cultures that engulf us. Our beliefs, actions and interactions are often a subset of culture. Cultural barriers are hidden just below the surface. If you know what they are, they are not usually barriers. When we think of culture we tend to think of foreign lands and faraway places, but culture is pervasive. It is part of organizations, families and corporations. It is spoken and unspoken.

The Internet records everything and forgets nothing. That is just the way it is currently on the digital frontier. Little attention has been given so far to ethics, privacy and life online. This is true for the workplace but is equally true for personal data. You can be long gone, to the great beyond, yet still thriving in cyberspace. Posting everything has become a really a big problem. One of the biggest issues is lack of awareness. What you are sharing? What is staying out there? Once something goes viral, it is literally everywhere (Baron, 2005).

In 2006, Stacy Snyder, then a 25-year-old student teacher at Conestoga Valley High School in Lancaster, PA posted a picture of herself on MySpace.com. It showed her at a party wearing a pirate hat and drinking from a plastic cup; the photo was captioned, "Drunken Pirate." Her supervisor told her it was unprofessional and the dean of education at Millersville University, where she was enrolled as a student, told her she was promoting drinking in virtual view of her underage students. The high school barred her from its campus. As a result, the university denied her a teaching degree because she did not finish her practicum, part of state requirements. Instead, it gave her a bachelor's degree in English. She sued, citing her First Amendment right to freedom of expression, claiming her actions were after-hours and perfectly legal. In 2008, the federal district judge rejected her claim, stating that she was denied her degree because she did not meet requirements. Moreover, the judge noted that teachers and public employees have First Amendment rights only on public matters and that the "Drunken Pirate" photo did not meet that definition. The photo had set off a chain reaction of events that derailed a young woman's career.

Every blog entry, Tweet, photo, status update and GPS coordinate can be stored indefinitely. Online chatter and ranting can come back to haunt the person posting it, months and even years later. I was speaking at a conference when a woman came to me and said, "I am in trouble. What can I do? During the presidential election, I was very passionate and behind one candidate and opposed to the other. I was out there, chatting it up on her blog. Well, my candidate won…but I lost my job. Now, when you Google me, I sound like some left-wing radical. I am trying to find a job. How can I get that information out of Google?" The tragedy of the Internet age is that both thoughtless bullies and innocent victims forget that privacy and identity go hand-in-hand. These rights are inalienable and used to be guaranteed in the free world by constitutional law, but somehow they have been usurped by technology, at least temporarily (Meece, 2011).

The reality of cyberspace is that you are being watched, literally, online and off. Digital fingerprints and footprints are stored forever. People have been fired from office jobs for complaining of boredom and from the NFL for making derogatory remarks about management. Every NCAA student athlete is warned not to post anything on Facebook you don't want in front of the Commissioner. Nearly 75 percent of human resource professionals say they are being asked by their companies to do online "research." Your presence can be researched everywhere: online gaming sites, Twitter, Facebook, Flicker, YouTube, and, of course, your personal website or blog (Heffernan, 2011).

In addition to presenting new threats to privacy, this also presents new threats to your psychological health. It is difficult to forget, forgive and move on when you are permanently archived in the Library of Congress. The Library of Congress has bought the Twitter files since 2006, and has decided to permanently archive them.

Facebook has more than 1 billion users, and Twitter has millions of folks tweeting. The average social media user creates 70 new pieces of content a month. All this chatting and collecting is leading to even more analyzing because the virtual environment has everything on the record (Rosen, 2010).

Cultural differences will always matter. How culture is defined and influenced is more fluid these days, thanks to technologies and connections. Now, instead of being defined by your ancestry, village, class or job, you are defined by your posts. Social mobility was once based on individualism and achievement, but now may be limited by social media. The idea of controlling your own identity in different segments of your life may be flawed. Influenced by friends, family, coworkers and neighbors, the idea of the segmented self has become unrealistic. You are no longer in control of your online identity unless you are aware of how this all works. Most people opt for public over private settings because public are more fun, more open, yet because of that carry the risk of being used in unethical ways – especially since the open or public data is being stored, sold and massaged in ways few of us understand. New industries are springing up to take care of our reputations online. They may wipe out what is stored in cyberspace, but we can't get our hands on it. For the virtual worker, the main point is awareness.

ARMED WITH A LOADED TECHNOLOGY ARSENAL

Thanks to the new technologies, society's collective unconscious is becoming more and more conscious. Technologies are merging together and re-emerging as new "mash-ups." GPS systems are joining with smartphone apps so that when you play games, there is a record of the game you played, time of the day when you played, street you were on and also who was in the living room with you when you played it. The number of apps, devices and web services you can use to connect seems almost infinite.

The importance of how you connect has shifted from what technologies you are using to how you are interacting with others. If you are open-minded and have the desire to try new things, you will have a much easier time being successful in the virtual environment. Similarly, having respect for others, a sense of humor, patience, tactfulness, humility, creativity, adaptability and appreciation will help also. So will tact, comfort with uncertainty, and flexibility. The most important change in connections, however, is a change in viewpoint.

This change is one of perspective, from "I" to "we." You need a multidimensional perspective to view the world and technologies that have opened up. Today, your identity depends less on the family or neighborhood you grew up in, the schools or church you attended, or even the country you call home, because you are being exposed to multiple viewpoints. You learn that there are many sides to an issue and different valid ways to think about things.

We are evolving from a "My Way" orientation to an "Our Ways" orientation. Still, it is difficult to ask people to expand their ways of interacting and connecting to others. It requires conscious and deliberate effort. We all want to fit in and we all want to feel secure. What we think we know, we hang onto. We are connecting more collectively.

The connections we make in the virtual workplace are much broader and more complex than the ones we made in the face-to-face environment. They are also much less private. We no longer communicate one-on-one or even one-on-many: we communicate many-to-many. This gives us a much broader exposure to diverse perspectives. As the arsenal of technologies increases, so do our connections. We can connect to more people in more ways. Yet with all this connecting, there is always a desire to connect in a way that establishes our identity, our importance and our acceptance. This is part of reinforcing our identity, who and what we are and how others perceive us.

Do I Wear a White Shirt?

There was a time not all that long ago that if you worked for IBM, you wore a white shirt. Not a pink shirt or a blue shirt, but a white shirt. It was a symbol of what was important: formality, establishment and detached professionalism. How quickly the world changed! We feel closer and more connected to the world around us via a variety of devices and gadgets. In contrast, we may not see another human being for extended periods of time. Now we are talking about wearing pajamas to work. That, too, is a symbol – of openness, freedom and relaxed proficiency. Knowing how to dress gave us a set of expectations. We expected ourselves to behave in certain ways when we put on the white shirt and we were expected to be able to elicit certain behaviors from others. IBM required that white shirt for a reason. Our priorities as individuals and as a global culture have changed. We live in a world where knowledge is everything. Ratings and postings have replaced hierarchies and structure.

Unknowingly, we gave away more than our symbols. We gave apps, websites and vendors the rights to stalk us, analyze us and interrupt us. We allowed the level of connection to increase and, with it, came an unprecedented increase in the noise in our lives. We convince ourselves that all this noise is necessary and that our privacy is secondary. Like Pavlov's dogs salivating, we check our email, posts and messages as soon as we hear the beep. We are obsessed with knowing. We want more information. We want to share because we want reassurance. We want feedback. We want to know that we are accepted, valued or even just OK. We are in danger or becoming addicted to our egos, our devices and to ourselves (Heffernan, 2011).

We gave away one of the greatest benefits of the industrial age, leisure time. In the agrarian age, no one had leisure time except the nobles, landholders and the elite. The industrial age gave us white shirts and vacation. It gave us the 9-to-5 workweek, instead of dawn-until-dusk. All this connectivity has taken away our ability to disengage. We feel we have to fill every minute with mental stimulus.

Using this new digital culture to our advantage means becoming comfortable from the inside out.

Aligning connections is about connecting on your terms, with your priorities and your responsibilities, so that you can get things done that are beneficial to you. This is not about egotism or self-esteem. It is about self-reliance and self-efficacy. It is about being able to believe in and act on your abilities, competencies and the right to be happy and thrive. Aligning connections puts you in charge of your destiny. You don't have to play a part and you don't have to wear a white shirt. You get to choose how much you are connected or how little, based on what you want to accomplish.

Aligning connections starts with an awareness of what you are doing. How are you connecting in the world of endless connections and what results are you achieving? If you are not connecting in a way that is beneficial to you, you get to fix that, change it and create connections that support your priorities. In a world where it is possible to be connected to the global Internet 24/7/365, you want to line up connectivity with productivity. This allows you to optimize your time, your talents and your involvement by supporting your intentions. Aligning connections is being challenged daily by new pulls, new technologies, and new ways to get noticed. Today it is one new technology; tomorrow it will be something else. Certainly, we are not going back to the cubicle and we are not going back to white shirts.

Meet Harry

Harry is a very talented and creative graphic designer. He runs his own independent business from his home. He loves what he does and he is good at it; that is, when he manages to get his projects to his clients on time. Harry has an old Mac and sometimes has software issues. He has all the software he needs to get the job done, but gets very upset when things don't go exactly as he thinks they should. Harry is constantly afraid that what he is producing is not good enough. He tries to do everything exactly as he learned it in school, but sometimes it just won't work. He is a perfectionist and wants it done right. He seems to always have an excuse why the project is not ready. What might help Harry be able to meet more project deadlines? How might he align his connections more effectively?

Meet Mark

Mark works for a global pharmaceutical company based in California. The company has production facilities in Austria and in the U.S. Mark has been asked to develop new marketing strategies for the European market but he does not understand much about it yet. When he contacted his Austrian colleagues via email, asking for help, Mark was inundated with email responses and ideas. However, he is having a hard time understanding what they mean, and he is frustrated with all the long emails back and forth. It appears that there is more than a time difference going on with this connection. What do you think is the problem? How can Mark better align his connections?

Meet Stan

Stan holds a Ph.D. in psychology and has had a 30-year career in organizational development. He has worked for some of the biggest and most well-known consulting agencies in New York City. Partially retired, Stan decided to teach online. He is neither very comfortable nor connected in this new environment. His students like him, because he is personable and knows his subject. He struggles with time and getting things done on time. Stan is always just barely getting things posted. He feels overworked and underappreciated. There is always a good reason, or so it seems, but he can't break out of this pattern of behavior. What suggestions might help Stan align his connections?

Respond-Ability Exercises: Aligning Connections

Exercise 1: Emotional Distance

Imagine you are a film director; mentally or actually write a movie script about your week. Give the main character (which is you) another name. Observe or witness what your character does. Watch the movie unfold from a distance. What do you see? How do you view you?

Exercise 2: How Are You Connecting?

For each of the following events, write how you would respond: by email, text message, video chat, social network post, phone call or face-to-face conversation:

You are not going to be able to meet your deadline.

You have a question and don't understand something at work.

Something good happened to you and you want to share it with everyone.

You just got yelled at and you feel terrible, so you want to tell someone.

Someone is doing something you don't like and you want to let that person know.

You have a personal announcement to make.

You just got a new job.

Something happened to someone you know and you want to tell someone else.

You are unhappy about something.

You want to tell your team of a new development.

You want to brainstorm a new approach.

You want to cancel a membership.

You received an email and you are angry and want to respond.

Someone is sick or has been injured.

Exercise 3: Connecting with Style

Look around your office or where you work at home. What do you see? What colors are there? What pictures? What images? Is it organized? Clean? Country or classic? Write down what you see. If you were going to design your own website, or if you already have a social network page, website or blog, what does it look like? What colors, images and attributes are there? This is how you communicate with and about yourself. This is a self-portrait of you. Even online, your style comes across. Think about this and reflect on the positive and negative aspects of how you may come across to others.

Exercise 4: Confident and Original

What color are you? Pick a color – one and only one color. Now describe yourself as if you were the color. Talk as if you were the color. Write down what you say, what that says about you, and how you connect? Are you bold and clear, mellow and bright, cool and detached?

Exercise 5: Digital Trails

How many emails do you currently have in your email accounts? How many email accounts do you have? How many websites, blogs, social network pages, text connections, devices? How long do you save conversations, postings or texts?? Do you email things from one of your accounts to another one of your accounts? How old is your oldest email? Why do you save it?

Exercise 6: Creating Connections that Support Success

How much uninterrupted time do you have in a day? Do you make appointments with yourself for exercise, the library, the back porch or a long drive? Are there days when you unplug totally? How many in the last month, last six months, last year? How does your mind work? Are you a different kind of thinker? Do you celebrate how you are unique? Do you let others be unique also? How do you label yourself and others? Do you look at your differences as gifts? How do you look at the differences of others?

Exercise 7: Imagine the Ideal Getaway

Imagine someplace where you can go to be alone together. Not a family vacation, not a sightseeing cruise, not an educational tour, but somewhere you can be with other people who are also getting away from the virtual world. What would you do? Play board games? Cards? Sports? Dance? Where would you be? How many people would be there? What part of the world would you be in? In vivid detail, write out the climate, setting and people you would bring into this escape. Maybe it is people you know and maybe it is total strangers. What would you have in common? What would you talk about? What would you do together?

9

Changing Respond-ability

"No one saves us but ourselves. No one can and no one may.
We ourselves must walk the path."

-- Buddha

Organizations are no longer defined by the limits of bricks and mortar. As individuals move to the virtual frontier, organizations benefit by supporting them. This empowers the individual and, in turn, furthers the goals and objectives of the organization. If individuals don't change, organizations can't change. Organizations, teams, corporations and institutions are made up of people. Clear expectations and limits help the virtual worker become aware of the organization's expectations, what is acceptable and what is not.

No one changes anyone who does not want to change. Leadership models and theory won't work if people are not inspired. In order to change, it is essential that individuals recognize and deal with challenges. It helps if they do not have to do this alone. Many times, especially in the virtual environment, workers are trying to deal with issues without much support. Meaningful and helpful encouragement from the organization and other individuals can increase the motivation. Performance evaluations and reviews, constructive feedback (both positive and negative) and support services can make all the difference.

Change in the Virtual Environment

Most individuals struggle with change at some time in their lives. For many years, the established scientific community told us we could not change as we got older because our brains were fixed. We became more and more hardwired and fixed in our ways. Thanks to neuroscience and research in recent years, we know this is not true. The term "neuroplasticity" describes changes in the brain caused by changes in behavior, environment, physical injury and neural processes. We now know that changes in the individual are possible. We also know that change begins with the individual being aware that it is necessary and then being motivated and supported to make that change. Very few individuals will make personal changes happen when they are comfortable. Psychologists will tell you that personal change usually comes about because something is not working for the person. Virtual workers want to be successful and enjoy both their lives and their work. They do not want to live in perpetual pain or be irresponsible workers.

It is important to be clear about ownership. Who owns the problem – is it an organizational problem or a personal problem? Taking ownership and taking responsibility for the outcome helps both the organization and the individual respond in ways that support success. If you can define what the issue is, and who owns it, then you can establish a way forward.

Virtual workers enjoy the virtual environment because it allows them more freedom. The challenge comes when the individual has to define where work ends and "me" begins. This ability to draw the line, to establish the boundaries of "me" or your identity, is a learned skill. You have been learning this since early childhood whether you realized it or not.

Having those critical conversations with others, setting up expectations and consequences ahead of time, and then following through with analysis and outcomes, determines who owns the respond-ability. Whether it is the individual or the organization, following through helps establish what is acceptable and not acceptable in the virtual environment. Some change is the responsibility of the individual. The organization can only offer you support and determine consequences if you refuse to change. Some change is the responsibility of the organization. Virtual workers need leadership within the organization to make those changes (Government eLearning, 2013).

It all begins with the awareness and willingness to recognize what is, then taking time to determine what you really want and take actions to achieve it. If something is happening in the virtual environment that you do not want – the boss expects you to be available 24/7, or you have no idea what is expected of you – it is your responsibility to "flip it." That means changing the situation from something you do not want to something you do want. It could be anything from your kids demanding all your time to your aged parents continuously intruding in your workspace. If you don't like something, or it isn't working for you, first become aware and then figure out what it is you do want or need. Part of being able to flip a situation is becoming aware and then being able to say "yes" or "no." Again, this applies to the organization as well as the individual.

"Yes" and "no" are difficult words. "No" is often seen as confrontational. It is the ultimate limit. Many people just do not want to deal with it. When we were children, we often confronted our parents when they said "no" and begged for a different response. Sometimes, it worked. Other times, we got the response, "What about 'no' don't you understand?" Yet "no" is a necessary word if you are going to function in the virtual environment, a place where you are already more vulnerable and more removed. Being able to say "no" is essential to setting your own boundaries and defining priorities. It is important to be able to say "yes," too. That is another difficult word. Many people can't say "yes" to their own preferences and priorities. That's why they may have priorities but they never get around to acting on them. "Yes" defines the other boundary or limit. What you say "yes" to, and what you say "no" to, defines how you respond and who you are.

Many things can influence your ability to say "yes" and/or "no," including your early upbringing, control, pressures, stress, personal and professional demands, anticipated or real needs and wants. Yet it is by defining who you are that you determine how successful you will be and what success looks like for you. There are many variations on this theme and psychology has a lot of great research regarding how to change your thinking, your emotions and your behaviors. This is a popular topic and books such as Daniel Kahneman's *Thinking Fast and Slow* provide well-researched evidence on why we humans do what we do.

RESISTANCE TO CHANGE

Success in the virtual environment requires more than just being aware of what you do. If you are not happy with what is going on, you need to respond differently. Collaboration, teams and interdependence begin with relationships. We build relationships with coworkers, family, friends and with ourselves. If you have not mastered the art of saying "no" and saying "yes," one of the first places it will show up is in your relationships. Online relationships are more fragile and more imaginary. It is easier to passively comply and inwardly resent. It is also easier to give in to pressure, either real or imaginary. Sometimes it comes from you and what you "should do" and sometimes from someone or something else. Either way, if you cannot say "yes" or "no" to internal or external pressures without guilt and anxiety, you have lost your ability to respond with autonomy. Autonomy requires self-control, of thoughts and then of actions. You define what you say "yes" to and what you say "no" to, both with your words and actions.

In the virtual environment, it is more difficult for people to believe where you stand when you do not use words that clearly define your intention. Your words let people know what you like and don't like. Without cues, it is important to be clear and concise. Letting people know what you like and what is unacceptable is one way that you define your relationships. You can make excuses and kid yourself as long as you want to but, eventually, to be happy and successful, you have to come to terms with the truth. You are already physically removed in the virtual world. Sometimes it is necessary to remove yourself emotionally to discover what is really going on. Taking time to be still and reflect can be a way of regaining autonomy. Sometimes you have to slow down to get a better perspective.

Emotional distancing can be challenging and difficult. If you feel unsafe or abused or insecure for any reason, it is important to take some emotional space. If you continue to set yourself up for disappointment and hurt, you will continue to experience those. One way forward is to give your heart and your head a break. You need to slow down to see things more clearly. This can be especially challenging with technologies that keep us constantly connected.

Fear is the biggest obstacle to personal change.
Overcoming fear is just being human. There are a lot of good reasons we have fears, but unnecessary fear causes problems in your life and is something you might want to address. When you are alone in the virtual environment, unnecessary fears can wreak havoc in your life. Before you can take steps to change them, you want to identify them and then take action. Some of these fears are so deeply entrenched into your subconscious that you believe they are facts.

The most common fear in humans is the fear of loss of love, or abandonment. Fear, not love, causes a great deal of doing and manipulating. These beliefs and entrenched subconscious patterns can go back to childhood. But if we are aware and willing to work, we can change them. Early in life, we may have learned that if we did not perform in certain ways, parents or people you depended on withdrew love. This sets up a pattern of doing or giving with resentment. So we give in to someone's requests or desires, and then feel like the victim. We resist being lonely and want to win over someone's love and affection or acceptance. When we don't, we see it as withdrawing love and support.

Anger is another common form of resistance to change. Some people can't tolerate someone else being upset with them. They look at it as a loss of love or abandonment. Other people hold on to their own anger because it gives them a sense of power and control. If they can't have what they want, at least they can have their anger. Anger usually causes stress; stress causes a whole range of undesirable conditions. It can pull virtual workers off task and out of flow, wasting time. If you respond with anger consistently, you are probably not focused on your priorities. After all, they are your priorities, not something you "have" to do. You will find yourself missing deadlines, becoming more frustrated and wasting a lot of time. If you have trouble staying on task and have too many diversions to take action on your priorities, you might want to examine the anger you feel.

Guilt is also a time-waster. Many people cannot say "no," so they say "yes" and then feel remorse or guilt. The motivation seems to be acceptance and sometimes people-pleasing. Mostly, they want to feel good about themselves. They want to be accepted and valued, so they say "yes" too much. Then they feel badly because they cannot always follow through or hold up their commitments. Saying "yes" to everybody and everything will interfere with your ability to respond by being authentically productive. You simply can't do it all – no one can. Sometimes you have to say "no." Yet people feel that by saying "yes" to everyone and everything, they can somehow overcome a sense of guilt inside and win approval.

Revenge is the feeling of a burden to pay back a wrong, or right an injustice. This is sometimes instilled in people in childhood or may be developed along life's journey. Revenge will interfere with your ability to respond by making responsible choices. When you feel a burden of always paying, and making others pay, it is a heavy load. It makes it difficult to make choices and be responsible to you. You feel you are always in debt or someone is in debt to you. This can show up financially, emotionally or even physically. You might actually struggle with debt or credit cards or you may feel the emotional burden of never feeling like you are good enough, have done enough or are doing enough. This can also show up as illnesses or maladaptive behaviors such as binging. Revenge causes people to feel they always have to pay back. It puts them under constant pressure.

Finally, the need for approval and acceptance will interfere with the ability to align connections. We see it every day: someone walking through the supermarket having an intimate conversation on a cellphone, a coworker constantly checking emails and text messages during a meeting, or someone who cannot stay away from a social networking site or massive online game. This is often an over-identification with others and under-identification with the self. Such people choose to live vicariously. They might be choosing to live through others because they have not dealt with their own negative emotions and disappointments. People who are constantly, yet inappropriately, connected do not want to be hurt; they crave recognition and immediate acceptance. Often, they are people-pleasers, who will go out of their way to gain approval. This often causes them to align their connections with others, but not necessarily with their own priorities. They are seeking immediate gratification. This makes it very difficult to align your connections.

How to Develop Respond-abilities

You have to be willing to change; if you don't want to, you won't. Even if you are willing, it is not easy to change behaviors and feelings that you have had for decades. Many people just refuse to deal with the behavior of the individual. They will sell you theories and models of leadership and organizational change but when it comes to changing individuals...too difficult! Organizations change because people are willing to change. Remember we said it is rare for people to change when they are comfortable. Change is usually something that happens in the individual because of structural tension. In other words, some part of their lives is not working.

To change a part of your life, you need to come to grips with what is currently happening. Not what you think is happening, or what you want to be happening, but what is currently happening. The best way to do this is to write. Writing works because it causes you to focus. You use dual tracks in the brain, audio and visual, and you can do it privately and reflectively. You can do this in many ways: by journaling, making lists, rerunning the movie of your life in your mind and taking notes, creating a cost-benefit analysis, or just writing down what you do all day. Use paragraphs or a chart – there is no right or wrong way to do this. But it is important to do it. Then put it away for a few days and reread it. Is it accurate? Are you being honest or are you deceiving yourself? Your brain can, and will, lie to you when you ask yourself to honestly look at your behaviors.

Next, you want to do the same thing with your thoughts. Thoughts are usually harder to describe realistically than behaviors. We have so many thoughts and they move very quickly through our minds. We tend to deceive ourselves when it comes to our thoughts. Neuroscience tells us that most humans think somewhere around 70,000 times a day. And here is the alarming part: 90 percent of those are repetitive thoughts. That is right – 90 percent! So if you are stuck in any life areas that are not working for you, you have lots of room for change. If you clean up just 10 or 15 percent of your thoughts, you will find your ability to act with autonomy drastically increased. You will be amazed.

It is important to become aware of what you are thinking. Again, writing is the best help. Make a list first thing in the morning of what your thoughts and feelings were yesterday. Thoughts and feelings go hand in hand. You don't think happy thoughts all day and feel depression. Be honest and take your time. Don't fool yourself. Do this for a week or more. Then look back at what you have written. Do you see any patterns of thought? What is not working that you want to work on? What do you want to change?

Do not assume these thoughts are reality. Reality is perceptual and relative. We all create our own version of reality as we construct our own thoughts. Even though things are real, we interpret them in our own way. It doesn't do any good to deny that things are real and that they happen. It does help to realize that you are the one interpreting people, circumstances and events, then constructing your own version of real. Reality is subjective, not objective, as you were taught in school. Shakespeare said, "...there is nothing either good or bad, but thinking makes it so." Try not to distort, judge, criticize or misrepresent, just write down your current thinking and then look for patterns of thought.

Now you want to "flip it" again. After you get a picture of what it is that you don't want, take a good look at what you do want. If you stay focused on what it is that you don't want, that will not help you respond with autonomy. Focus on what you want to change and what you want to create. To act with autonomy, you have to be able to think with autonomy. If you are experiencing emotional pain, hurt, discomfort or displeasure, ask yourself if you want to hang on to it or get over it. Many people will hang on to deep emotional pain for years or lifetimes. But it is a choice. If it is really difficult, you might want to get professional help, which is not a problem. You always have the choice to work on you. That is what acting with autonomy is all about – being able to respond independently, the way you choose to respond.

One important point with creating change: write what is currently happening. Then write down what you want to change. Choose the results you want and then move on to something else. Do not dwell on this or try to force change. If you focus too much on what is going wrong, your mind will make sure it continues. This is also not a once-and-done. Reflection is an ongoing process and repetition is very effective in learning. When changing, which is not always easy, what you are trying to do is tip the balance of power to a new direction.

Psychologists have lots of tools and techniques to help you do this. There are a variety of worksheets that are free on the *The Pajama Effect* website (http://www.thepajamaeffect.com). The last 50 years of psychology has concentrated on cognitive, rational and emotive therapy. Most people are not really into Freud anymore. Even fields like Neuro-Linguist Programming (NLP) focus on change your thoughts, change your thinking and change your actions. So approach changing your respond-abilities with an attitude of intention, ease and commitment.

Very few folks make significant changes the first time they attempt the process. The idea of a lightning bolt miracle occurring and your life being changed forever usually happens only in the movies. There is no magic in this but there is science. Neuroscience and brain mapping tell us that if you want to learn new things, you need new neuroanalytic pathways. The more well-worn the pathways, the more difficult, but not impossible, it is to make changes. Neuroplasticity research tells us that the brain is adaptive; it can and will change. Practice is very important to success, so stay positive with yourself. The brain releases chemicals every time you think and feel. If you strengthen the negative, guess what you are getting more of?

We have learned a great deal in the last few years, thanks to innovations in brain research and advancements in technologies. One thing we have learned is that negatives affect both the listener and the speaker. Drama causes chemicals to be fired off in the brain. This is why we are bombarded with disaster and drama on television. If it's the weather channel reporting tornados a continent away or two politicians engaging in negative mudslinging campaigns, what you put into your mind sticks, whether we believe it is true or not! It is also the reason that pharmaceutical ads have couples walking hand in hand and beautiful people rowing a boat on the lake at sunset, just before they reel off pages of disclaimers on how their drugs may cause harm. What you hear and see sticks, unless you replace it with something else. When you are making changes, be careful to focus on what you want.

In the virtual workplace, you are much better off taking 15 minutes to be in silence than succumbing to an online distraction. Try to stay or get to a point of relaxation. Again, there is a lot of literature on present-moment awareness and relaxation responses. Meditation is one way folks achieve this. Distraction by watching TV, playing games or watching movies is another. When working virtually, be aware of and watch out for distractions – games, shows, chat rooms and social networks, to name just a few. Focused attention is much stronger than passive attention. You decided to play solitaire to relax at lunchtime and now it is 3:30 p.m. What happened? You fell into detached attention. You are not paying attention to what you are doing. When you are focused on something, even breathing, you are aware.

Watch out for anger. It gives a false sense of confidence and optimism. You don't want to repress it either. This just pushes anger inward to the subconscious. A great deal of research has been done on the links between repressed anger and disease. None of it shows repressed anger to be healthy! If you are angry and that is one thing you want to change, try slowing everything down. Step outside yourself and watch whatever it is you are angry at as if it was a movie. You are on the outside, looking in. Still angry? Try the old silent-movie approach by rerunning your movie, but very slowly and very overdone. If nothing else, you might start taking it all less seriously. Now think about something you want. You can only think one thought at a time. You cannot think about what you do want and what you don't want simultaneously.

Most of the negative self-talk that is derailing you is patterned speech, causing feelings and behaviors to follow. It is like running an old movie over and over and over. It is wordy and familiar, so if you derail it by slowing the self-talk down and exaggerating the action, you have a better chance of interrupting the pattern. Which is exactly what you are trying to do, interrupt the old patterns long enough and often enough to install new ones. These new patterns are more aligned with your ability to succeed in the virtual environment.

If you are looking for behavioral change models you can find pictures, lists and charts everywhere. If you really want to change, stay away from labels and models. Most of these will not help you. What will help you is developing your own game plan and setting short-term achievable goals that have consequences, both positive and negative. One thing that is missing in the virtual world is positive reinforcement from others. The ability to celebrate and enjoy things with others is different online. So while you are going through the process of focusing on success in the virtual workplace, give yourself some time to celebrate. Give yourself lots of positive feedback and reinforcements.

Celebrate Success

These respond-abilities will help you be happier and more successful working virtually. As you begin to eliminate past programming and to think with autonomy, reward yourself. Setting and enacting your priorities is something that is beneficial to all aspects of life. Being authentically productive will help you lead in the virtual environment and realize your personal goals as well. Making responsible choices frees you from self-sabotage. Aligning your connections lets you meet your own needs as well as the needs of your job. When you take responsibility for your own life and how you respond to others, you quit making excuses and you stop being a victim of circumstances.

It is important to understand that success in your job is up to you, especially in the virtual environment. There usually is no one else there to intercede. Your life and how you blend it is your responsibility: you schedule, you act and you produce. If you say "yes" and you really mean "no," eventually it will come out. You will be resentful and make excuses. An internal "no" wipes out an external "yes" every time! When you make a commitment to yourself and stick to it, you are acting with autonomy and overcoming compliance. Give yourself credit when you are successful. After all, you deserve it.

Do not ignore your feelings. Emotions have a purpose. They are a signal that has a function. Anger, fear and sadness all tell you that something is out of balance. Whether it is about a work issue or a personal problem, these emotions are part of who you are for a reason. Be glad you have them and acknowledge their message. The power of anger is to tell you that somewhere you are giving up autonomy. You are making or letting someone else have control of your life. Anger is a secondary emotion and the underlying emotion is usually fear. Fear is a warning to move away from threat. Ask yourself: What is being threatened? Is this fear real or imagined? If it is real, take responsibility for responding to it. Sadness is always a sign of loss. If you have lost an opportunity, a relationship or a raise, remember it is your responsibility to respond in a way that is beneficial to you. When you can, celebrate your victories and know that your confidence and autonomy will benefit.

If you are going to be authentically productive, you cannot go around rescuing other people, whether they are your kids, your parents or your fellow workers. You need to stay on task. This requires personal discipline and personal project management skills. Personal project management gets easier when you work at it. You develop your own your critical path and you stay on it. If you get off the path, make the adjustments necessary. Be sure to schedule and take time off. Overworking, overachieving or overdoing will cause burnout. Even if you feel obligated to do so, resist the urge to do more. More is a message that is prevalent in Western cultures and the pressure is everywhere. Online, when the days never end and work is blended with play, you have to draw limits and set boundaries for yourself. When you achieve this, celebrate your successes. When you don't, reboot. It is never too late to take control of your life.

Making responsible choices is about taking your power back. If you have given too much power to your boss, your family or the social network, you can change that. When you let go of excuses, blame and projection, you take your power back. This is a big step because you stop lying to yourself and start being honest. The willingness to make improvements is what makes the difference. A social support system will help. Friends can be helpful also. This is where the company can step in and make it easier for the virtual worker by sponsoring classes and collaborative sessions that support people in changing and growing. Forget the condemnation and criticism. Create collaborative groups where people can establish bonds and attachments. Everyone needs a friend at work.

The ability to respond in the virtual environment is the difference between being in control of your destiny and being at the mercy of everyone and everything else. You have a choice. You can be the person in power and get what you want or you can play the victim. Excuses are cheap in the virtual world; in fact, they are free, but they do not help you gain autonomy. They do not help you become successful and they do not help you take control of your life. If you are dissatisfied, tell someone. Do not sit and stew over it internally. Do not try to overcompensate.

Resentment and attempts to control the uncontrollable are sure signs that you need to re-examine the way you are responding. If you are the team member who is attempting to do it all, back off. It is not your responsibility to do everything; you only need to do your job. By trying to do it all, you are trying to either rescue someone or control someone. That will not benefit you in the virtual workplace. When you feel resentful, it is a warning that the connection is not mutual. Aligning your connections is a mutually beneficial response. You can't connect with someone else if they do not want to connect to you. Don't punish yourself; just do your job and let someone else know your situation. Do not sit in isolation and fret. Reaching for others to support us is what aligning our connections is about. When we set and enact our priorities, aligning our connections lets us achieve our goals.

Remember, when you work virtually, you are working in an environment where most of the boundaries of the traditional workplace have vanished. You need to be more determined than ever to be in charge of your life. The benefits are more productivity, more autonomy and the ability to balance your life the way you desire, not on someone else's terms. The challenges are many and this is very new. Never in the course of human history has so much change happened so quickly. The change is still coming. We are all still adapting to this and we are still enveloped by an increasing rate of change. New devices, new ways to connect and new connections make the virtual environment a bit like the Wild West. The rules are evolving and we are all adapting to a new world.

10

Leading in the Virtual Environment

"When one door of happiness closes, another opens; but often we look so long at the closed door that we do not see the one which has been opened for us."

--Helen Keller

Supporting the virtual workforce in the 21st century will require organizational effort. The challenge to business is very real. How do we support virtual workers and hold them accountable when we can't observe their behaviors? Ineffective management will leave you totally at a loss. How do you manage people you cannot see? Management used to be able to tell you were a hard worker because you were in the cubicle every night until 8:30 p.m. Now, no one knows.

The meanings of the words "management" and "leadership" have been debated for a number of years, but in most companies not much has really changed. Skilled leaders with vision still make all the difference. Business is not going back to the cubicle. It is ineffective, inefficient and costs this planet enormously to have everyone commuting long distances to work. We pay in smog, gasoline, lost time, carbon emissions, pollution, wars and global warming. The costs of the age of the automobile are real. The time has come to pay the piper.

"To become the absolute best place to work, communication and collaboration will be important, so we need to be working side-by-side. That is why it is critical that we are all present in our offices. Some of the best decisions and insights come from hallway and cafeteria discussions, meeting new people, and impromptu team meetings. Speed and quality are often sacrificed when we work from home. We need to be one Yahoo! and that starts with physically being together" (King, 2013). A memo from Yahoo management put virtual workers on notice, but even Yahoo can make mistakes. It is very possible to work side by side virtually. The remote worker can be more collaborative and more productive but the leadership needs to know how to make that possible. When this announcement came out, there was an immediate backlash of folk who said this was Yahoo's way of cutting an overly bloated staff and trimming down the bottom line. If it were true, that would be sad. Businesses can learn to support a workforce in the 21st century.

The real issue is: why aren't companies helping people work together virtually? Why don't companies know what performance is expected and acceptable from virtual employees? Physical presence is only a minor part of this problem. Certainly, in the age of social networking and global interactions, the issue is not the ability to connect. Virtual workers have very few support services, but their needs as human beings are as important as ever. The answer to change in human performance lies in addressing and supporting change in human behaviors.

In the virtual world, workers still need to show up and be held accountable. It is management's job to set those expectations. Leaders need the authority to take action. If employees are productive, reward them. If they are not, take the action necessary: implement improvement plans, have the hard conversations and, if necessary, release them. Bringing virtual employees back to the office doesn't get rid of poor leadership practices. Both management and the employees need to understand that working in the virtual environment is still *working*. In order to do a job well, you have to give it your attention. You cannot be changing laundry, babysitting, caregiving or engaged in a multitude of other distractions and be productive. You have to show up on time and on task.

Working productively in the virtual world requires accountability, trust and performance. It is the job of organizational leadership to set the expectations for high performance: determine how often to meet, call on clients, do site visits, report information and whatever else it takes to get desired results. The responsibility to define and administer performance criteria belongs to the company's leadership. Leadership needs to define and clearly communicate these performance expectations by establishing a clear purpose, common vision, business objectives and measurable outcomes.

There is no shortage of communication venues in the virtual world, but there can be a lack of real communications. It is the job of leadership to establish communications channels and make sure that they are kept open. Results are what matter, so company leadership needs to set the framework for how, when and what those successful results will look like. Then, leadership must effectively communicate that framework to everyone. Collaborating online works and good leadership works to make sure everyone knows they are an important and respected part of the team (Davis, 2013).

THE IMPORTANCE OF CLEAR PURPOSE

Employers have a need to know that their employees are performing effectively and efficiently. Some employers will require virtual workers to show up in the office at least a few days a week. In most cases, it is a token gesture. Face time visits give the employer a sense of control and the employee a physical and social presence. Does it increase performance or productivity? Probably not. Most virtual workers will tell you they visit the office for political reasons. They actually get more done at home. Schlepping to the office wastes a lot of time.

Technology has given us a different clock. We can always be connected. The communications are the challenge, not the connection. If you can't manage by observation anymore, and the 40-hour workweek doesn't exist, how can you keep track of work time? Work time has been replaced by performance and accomplishments. It is leadership's job to set very clear objectives and communicate them effectively. These clear objectives must have accountability built in. They have to be marching orders, not a passive position statement. The balanced scorecard approach needs to apply to the individual and not just the C-Suite (BalancedScoreCard.org, 2013).

Smart people work best when they know what success looks like. This in no way stifles innovation or creativity. It does provide a vision and an expectation of success. Smart people like to know what is expected of them and then be given the resources, authority and flexibility to make it happen. Top performers will do backflips to meet and exceed the company's expectations, but those expectations have to be communicated. Working in the virtual world requires a level of communication detail beyond what is needed in the face-to-face world. A smile and a handshake are not going to do it in the virtual environment. The virtual environment has too much space and details can easily fall through the cracks. Leadership must communicate clearly what the expectations are for performance and what the consequences are if those expectations are not met (Gupta, 2013). The biggest challenge to the 21st-century workplace is the transition from face-to-face supervisor to remote leader. It is not people working in their pajamas. It is not getting a culturally diverse virtual team to collaborate. It is not the lack of face-to-face spontaneity or efficacy. It is learning how to lead people in this new workplace by giving people the support, resources and backing they need to succeed.

Remote leadership occurs when the supervisor cannot see and observe the employees and their work processes. The challenges of working in the virtual world do not just affect the virtual worker; they also affect the leadership of the organization. Clear expectations, directions, time constraints, cultural and language issues, and disconnects between how work gets done and how it gets rewarded, should be documented and made clear to all concerned.

COMMON VISION

A common business vision begins with trust. If there is no trust in where you are going, how can you believe you are going to get there together? Trust is multidimensional and all-important in the virtual environment. Employers must trust their employees and workers must trust their bosses. This was difficult in the office environment and the discord between labor and management in the capitalist system is legendary. Each side is supposed to have conflicting interests, one side against the other. But this divided consciousness, this difference in interests, cannot be sustained in the virtual world. There needs to be a buy-in and common vision that is mutually beneficial to everyone.

The reason management had to watch everyone at work, or clock them in and out, is because workers could not be trusted to do the job. It was a management-against-labor world. The communication was from the top down.

Trust is always an issue in virtual management. You need to be more accountable, more adaptable and less offensive. The rule of thumb is to be specific in what you want and how you express it. You want to be light and fun, but watch the humor. Like sarcasm, humor can easily be misunderstood, so it might be best to avoid it altogether (Roebuck & Britt, 2002).

Communication is very important in a common vision. Social networks, crowdsourcing and the Internet have drastically changed the way we communicate with each other and the way we spread information. This, in turn, has changed the way we think about power. Advancements in technology continue to make it easier and easier to communicate with each other. At the same time, these communications are less and less private. Everyone knows at least one story of a famous person who has been caught sending sexually explicit photos electronically. Everyone also knows what it is like to be watched. You go on a website and the following week you begin to receive emails for the same kind of product as the one you were searching for on the Internet. Most of us understand that our communications online are anything but private. Communications are both less private and more horizontal than they were in the past. So, to communicate a common vision, it has to be one that everyone buys into and respects.

What productivity looks like also needs to be defined and communicated. This has become very challenging in the age of the knowledge worker. It was easy to count widgets, containers or tons and know what productivity looked like, but when the commodity is ideas and knowledge it becomes a lot more difficult. This requires clear analytics and objectives to be defined early on by the organization's leadership and then clearly communicated to employees. No one can be held accountable for productivity and performance if they don't know what that means. Realistic and affirmative expectations and metrics are important in defining and measuring productivity.

So leadership, in the world of the virtual worker, needs to make some decisions about business direction, common objectives and employee performance support. Certainly, in the age of "big data," the information and tools exist to analyze just about anything. None of that really matters, however, if we don't do it. And this cannot be a token superficial effort. Managing people in the virtual environment will take some real initiative from the top and all the way through the ranks. It will require looking at those things your organization may not want to look at, like defining what you want from your employees and why and how you expect to get it. Most importantly, leading in the virtual environment requires trust. Trust is a two-way street that includes defining and communicating what is expected and then supporting people, not commanding them.

EXPECTATIONS AND A ROAD MAP

Communications can be challenging in any work environment. It can be downright perplexing in the virtual environment. If you look at literature on virtual teams, it focuses on issues of trust and relationships between team members. Some will report cultural differences, conflicts in management styles or leadership challenges. But most difficulties arise because there is a gap. There are people on a team who have come together to get a job done but just do not know what to expect or what's expected of them. Because of the distance, the space and the anonymity in virtual communications, trust can be an issue.

The physical space between team members can affect how these people interact. A multitude of technologies have sprung up to allow us to feel closer and collaborate. But that is not all that has happened; organizations have become more global and much flatter. The rules have changed and so have hiring expectations. Organizations can optimize expertise by hiring from a diverse workforce, matching the right person with the right job, and finding workers anywhere in the world. But virtual workers and teams cannot become invisible. The virtual workforce needs to be highly visible and supported right from the start.

Organizational leadership can set the performance expectations, and promote and support the virtual office, using a hands-on approach of establishing and creating effective working agreements. These agreements can be discussed and used to convey expectations of the organization and the employee. Working agreements can also convey support, training and the accountability expected by everyone. These virtual workplace agreements might be structured like contracts with buy-in from both sides.

Virtual performance agreements need to communicate clear expectations, business objectives, performance goals and measurements. For example:

> The purpose of this business is to ......[State clearly in operational terms.]
>
> Our values include .... [State clearly in operational terms]
>
> We demonstrate these values by ..... [State clearly in operational terms]
>
> ....so that these business objectives can be obtained: ....[List objectives and how the outcome will be measured] (Becker, Ballentine, Tedford & Lee, 2001).

For example: The purpose of Protector Insurance Inc. is providing international insurance products that offer quality protection with reasonable pricing. The individuals who work as part of this organization value our clients, our staff members, and our insurance companies, and respect the interests and goals of each group. We demonstrate those values through respect, trustworthiness and integrity in our dealings with each other and our clients. We measure success by our customers choosing us because they believe in our ability to meet or exceed their expectations of value, service and knowledge.

Next, list the objectives and make them measurable. Use verbs and quantitative measures where possible. Create statements that provide specific, realistic, practical and measurable objectives and actions. There is no room for anything vague here.

For example:

- The sales department members will communicate with each other at least twice a week.
- All customer communications will be handled in a timely manner, with response given within 48 hours.
- A 30-minute progress meeting will be held each Monday at 3 p.m. EST and everyone is expected to attend.
- Each week, progress reports will be reviewed on Friday and written recommendations sent out on Monday by 9 a.m.

These must be specific, not general, statements. They are the standards you want to establish for your organization and you want everyone's buy-in. Sometimes it will even require you to make up your own definition of terms. The important thing is, don't take anything for granted or assume. Make it clear, make it measurable and make it specific. The more clearly the expectations are defined, the easier it is to eliminate miscommunications.

Leading in Constant Change

In the virtual world, you want to establish and adhere to communication norms. To share critical information, collaborate and get the job done, you do not want to leave anything to chance. Good communication skills in the virtual world are a learned art. You must have personal contact in a very impersonal environment, so you need to be more articulate, share more personally and celebrate success.

Virtual leadership gains its strength by organizing distant team members to accomplish specific goals. We used to assume that allegiance was temporary. As more of us continue to move toward virtual work, the transitory aspects of the virtual environment are vanishing. Virtual work is a way of life. It is the way we work and will work in the 21st century. Work will come to the pajama worker; the pajama worker will not have to go into the office to work. This means more flexibility, informality, enhanced autonomy and innumerable other benefits. It also means it is a more challenging environment for leadership (Beck et al. 2001).

Distance magnifies dysfunction. Influence and rules are more difficult to impose with miles, time and distance between us. Human relationships can be strained when distance and time divide us: ask anyone who has tried to carry on a long-distance love relationship. This same divide affects virtual teams and virtual management. When you are away from others, change can be magnified and change in the virtual world is constant.

Change can come quickly and sneak up on those who aren't expecting it. In the pajama workplace, it is not just about managing people or projects but also about managing change, both professional and personal. The digital boss must exert influence and assume responsibility for challenges over great distances while confronting a very competitive and often hostile environment (Davis, 2008). Everything and everyone can compete for the worker's attention.

Leadership is the use of power and influence to change and direct our behaviors and the behaviors of others. Leadership is energy, engagement and trust. First, a leader needs to have the confidence and know-how to manage himself or herself. Then the leader must establish trust and reliance.

Leadership in the virtual world is not about digital spying. It is not about monitoring every move, although this is totally possible because everything is digital and can be tracked. Some companies require employees to use continuously running video surveillance cameras. Have you heard of the microchips they put in puppies – maybe we are next? The surveillance gurus can already track us by GPS if they want to, so long as we have the device with us. In the last 10 years, cameras have been installed everywhere: at red lights, in hotel lobbies, at the bank, in the grocery store and at the gas station. We are constantly being recorded and monitored and all this "big data" is being used.

Fear has never been a good way to lead. Effective skills for nourishing relationships and supporting interactions need to be supported by senior managers who understand and appreciate the nuances and skills needed to lead at a distance. Support from the top is everything and must be given in a non-threatening, straightforward way. Organizational systems need to be upgraded and adapted to accommodate the stresses and strains of working virtually. There is a fine balance between the invisible digital boss and the intrusive one. The boss who is always intervening doesn't allow for autonomy, doesn't have the respect of the team and is not cultivating collaboration. Resentment and dependence are more likely to result. This then becomes a downward spiral of lack of trust and no one benefits. Uncertainty in the digital world can make everyone on edge. This is almost always a sign of poor leadership.

CREATING CULTURE AND OPPORTUNITIES

Cultural differences do not just exist between people from various countries or those living on separate continents. Such differences can exist within geographical boundaries, organizations and companies. Cultural differences become important to consider when they create a mismatch of meaning. If the culture is Western, it is probably more interested in facts, deadlines and data. If it is Eastern, perhaps group relationships and roles are more important. Losing face and problem solving are dealt with differently in varying cultures. Hierarchies of roles and authority have culture-specific meanings. Awareness helps you understand these clashes. Education and training can help overcome cultural gaps, but so can creating a new virtual culture that is unique to your team or organization.

Before the virtual workplace, when we went to work we checked our culture of origin at the door. We assumed the corporate culture and we took on its DNA. We internalized the expectations, meaning and behaviors necessary to succeed. Now, the organization must convey to the virtual worker the values, mission and purpose of the business. Each role must be defined as to what constitutes appropriate interactions, and when.

Establishing norms and rules that serve your unique virtual community helps to establish unique bonds. Success in the virtual world takes a strong commitment. The job of remote leadership is to communicate the mission, get commitment to the vision and to each other.

Leadership has a great deal of responsibility. The leadership is responsible for setting the tone of interactions. If leaders are untrusting, disorganized or unyielding, virtual workers might reflect the same. Clarity is essential to the virtual worker. Clarity begins with a clear sense of self and purpose. This clear purpose enables virtual workers to take timely and appropriate action. All personal requirements, selfish motives and individual perspectives are inconsequential if the mission and purpose are clear.

Unclear communications and misunderstanding can happen easily with everyone sitting around a conference table. When you have people in far-off places, different time zones and multiple native languages, the situation can be even more challenging. It is important that you give the person who is speaking your attention…total attention. Misunderstanding and miscommunication are more common when attention is unfocused. When communicating with others, background or back-channel tasks and conversations are not helpful to you or the goal.

Let go of all distractions and focus your attention on listening. Do not try to answer the question or rebuke the argument before you have heard it. This is a normal human tendency and one that is very prevalent in people who are primarily visual. Stop trying to answer the request, formulate a response, create a counterargument or tell a new story. Staying focused and listening will increase clarity of purpose and cement goals and objectives that are essential to success in the virtual environment.

Clarity enables you to feel secure in knowing what is expected of you. To perform at an effective level, you must trust that your leadership will do what they say they will do, when they say they will do it. In the virtual world, trust is everything. Because the normal visual and sensory cues have been removed, one must rely on intuition, that "sixth sense." Trust reduces misunderstandings, hurt feelings and broken commitments. In an atmosphere of trust, when these do arise and are discovered, they can be dealt with openly and honestly. Harboring distrust, resentment and ill feeling can go on for a long time in the virtual world. It can take much longer to see a problem or an issue in the isolation and solitude of miles and anonymity.

Virtual environments require people to reach out from their heads and their hearts. They have to make an effort to connect, support and reassure. An ounce of prevention will set things in order before the confusion begins. In the words of Lao Tzu, founder of Tao philosophy, "Deal with it before it happens. Set things in order before there is confusion. A journey of a thousand miles begins with one step."

Timing is also important in the virtual environment. Time cannot be taken for granted or wasted. All work has a life cycle and needs to be done in a timely manner. Nothing needs to drag on indefinitely or endlessly. The technologies should always be used to support the business purpose with as effortless and transparent an action as possible. Technologies need to be used to encourage and strengthen relationships and influences. They should never be the center of the discussion.

PROTOCOLS IN A VIRTUAL WORK ENVIRONMENT

"No, you can't call me at home at 10 p.m. on a Friday night." Everyone has limits. You have to be able to set yours. There is a lack of standards and protocols in the virtual environment so you and your teams must create your own. It is more than just practical to take into account every team member's times, schedules and needs – it is a necessity. Schedule in advance. Make sure everyone knows when she or he is expected to be connected and keep to the schedule.

Protocols often appear to be opposites:

- You need leadership to handle the inertia and the distance, but that same leadership wants to impose limited structure and control.

- You need a well-thought-out plan to manage the project, the team and the individuals. Such plans must be fluid and flexible but also highly accountable to achieve the goals of the business.
- Business objectives come before the individual, but the individual's needs must be met.
- Expectations and roles must be clear, but these roles need to be flexible enough to adjust as situations change.
- You want to be able to balance changes without forcing answers.
- The opinions of others must be respected, acknowledged and merged into a solution, even if there is struggle.
- Criticism and conflict should be avoided and results cannot be forced.

Learning together and improving together is also very important. Just as with flight crews and surgical teams, virtual workers must be focused on excellence. Continuous learning, sharing and improving will also help nurture new norms and ideas. Training for the virtual environment must necessarily address the needs of both the individual and organization. Organizations are made up of individuals who play a part and make a contribution. It is the job of leaders to support the virtual worker as part of the 21st-century workforce. Organizations need to re-examine performance and make a shift toward defining expectations that will replace observation.

Transparency and Limiting Options

There are all kinds of options for collaboration and communication in the virtual environment – so many that it can be overwhelming. For everyone to function effectively, it is wise to limit the number of tools used. You need the technology to be transparent so individuals can focus on the purpose and content. It helps if the participants learn to use the technologies really well, so well that they do not have to focus or think about using them.

It is important for all virtual workers to be trained, feeling confident and comfortable using whatever tools will be used for team communications. The easier the tools are to use, the more valuable they become to creating a transparent conversation. It is important to have technical support available whenever anyone anywhere needs it. This gives a sense of security and belonging. Often teams find it valuable to have face-to-face meetings, especially when several new team members come on-board. If this is not possible, a virtual social event of some sort can help the members become familiarized with the technologies and with each other. Make it fun, make it personal and make it easy.

A general feeling of knowing where you are and what is expected of you is important for virtual workers. Leadership should strive to communicate well-defined goals and objectives as well as ways of evaluating performance and assessing success. Standardizing tools will also help set priorities that can then be acted upon.

Having common and limited technologies lessens the anxiety of communicating in the virtual workspace.

A lot of folks are not going into the office anymore. A study by the Telework Research Network showed a 75 percent increase in telework from 2005 to 2011, while the overall workforce grew only by 4.3 percent. Leadership is needed to support these workers. How you manage a workforce you cannot see and observe must evolve to meet this need (Massie, 2013). It is a precarious situation because many companies don't have the technologies, infrastructure or systems and security to support remote workforces.

Good leadership has always been about vision – the vision of what is required to be successful now and a vision of the organization's future requirements. Many organizations already know that telecommuting cuts costs and that the productivity of most virtual workers is much greater than for employees working in the office. What is needed is more support for the individual and more support for the whole person. Support doesn't just mean more technologies; it also includes psychological, administrative and learning support.

Leading in a virtual workplace is about respecting, inspiring and trusting people. Good leaders always seem to know that the secret to their success is to hire the right people, get them in the right positions and then get out of the way and let them do their jobs. If you give them the support they need, a clear vision and objectives, and have those crucial conversations, good people will come through most of the time. Good leaders know how to stay close and be there for their people and yet not be intrusive or domineering.

Hands-off and laissez-faire management is not going to work in the virtual environment. Those approaches make it far too easy to get lost. Without respect, people do not feel appreciated. People who are not appreciated usually have low motivation. Without inspiration, how can there be any creativity and innovation? Without trust, there will never be dedication. Leading in the virtual environment requires leaders with compassion, imagination and commitment. Every virtual worker has to be their own leader in their own environment.

Many people would argue that the technologies of this new century have ushered in an age where respect has been forgotten. Media floods us all day long with images of the worst things about humanity. It trivializes and sensationalizes. It presents pictures of a world possessed by violence, scripted reality and disrespect. Respect used to be about respecting authority for the sake of authority. But in the "flat world" of the 21st century, where social networks rule our views of collective consciousness, respect has taken on a different meaning. Perhaps it has not been forgotten but just repositioned. A person with strong leadership skills must be empowered, and empower others, to accomplish great things. Leaders want to see the best in others and in themselves. Respect begins with honesty. Respect for oneself and for others creates awareness and acceptance.

The old way of thinking was: you can't trust employees. When the cat is away, the mouse will play, went the old thinking. But what was missing here was visible accountability. In order to trust people, you need to make expectations clear, then support people and hold them accountable. You can't get to innovation without inspiration. To lead, you need to be inspired to get the job done and dedicated to the priorities you set down for yourself. You want to be committed to making yourself better and helping those you work with become better.

COLLECTIVE INDIVIDUALITY

Howard Rheingold, a thinker and writer on the digital world, described the Internet as the greatest social experiment ever. All this technology has brought us the ability to analyze a collective consciousness. As individuals, we use technologies to connect, communicate and carry on our lives. As a global community, we have created a vast amount of data that can be analyzed and re-analyzed to reflect the state of human awareness. The tasks we are asked to perform are more complex and we are more reliant on others to be able to accomplish those tasks. The mundane and the repetitive are being automated. Computers, robots and other technologies are taking away responsibilities and jobs.

Managing the 21st-century workforce is about more than details like being on time, clear communications and follow-through. Important and admirable as these characteristics are, they reflect process not creativity. The industrial age was about efficient process but the new workplace is about independence and innovation. The age

254

of the pajama worker is one of interdependent individuals, connected together by a common vision. These workers rely on each other but are independently motived to educate themselves and prepare for the next wave of change. Continuous learning is part of what they do to have a better today and tomorrow.

We connect as individuals but the totality of our connections brings us closer as human beings. It is easy to see we are more alike than we are different. It is easier to share our feelings, our humanity and our failings. It is much easier to accept our faults if we have collective evidence that we are not the only ones that have them. Our mistakes don't seem so threatening when we know millions of others have made the same mistakes. This collective consciousness gives us a new perspective on what it is to be human and our place in the world. It also makes us more responsible as individuals because we can see how each thought, each conversation and each response contributes to the bigger conversation.

The virtual workplace is here to stay. Businesses are not going back to the cubicle. The world's dependence on oil, levels of pollution, global warming and commute times will help to usher in what technology has enabled. Our ability to work in our pajamas enables us to look at life and human interactions differently. *The Pajama Effect* is a psychological and behavioral shift in response to a new way of life. The age of hunting and gathering, the agrarian age and the industrial age have given way to the pajama age. It is the age of the remote connection, of human interactions with technologies and of virtual everything. We work online, we play online and we shop online.

Our workplace has changed. The way we measure value is no longer the number of widgets produced. The commodities that ruled the age of manufacturing – the hours you worked, the times you punched in and out, and the observation of management – have given way to a new way of looking at the world. Gone are the time sheets, dress codes and structure of the workplace. The virtual workplace promises to be much more productive and a whole lot more fun. Creative ideas and innovation have become more important to us than commodities. No one wants to be just another company. No one wants to be just another employee.

A new set of skills is important for affecting this virtual work environment. Success requires people who can think, live and work with autonomy. Gone are the days when compliance ruled. This new environment is different. We are alone a good bit of the time with ourselves yet connected to just about everything, just about all of the time. The devices that connect us become obsolete in six months and are replaced every 13 months. The rate of change is accelerating. We have "thinking things" connected to a semantically aware Internet. From deciding when to turn on our air conditioning to suggesting what movies we might like to watch, these devices are getting smarter. Everything is being recorded. Everything is digital.

There are cameras everywhere. If you run a red light or forget to stop at the tollbooth, you are recorded. If you are shopping in a store or doing business at the bank, you are recorded. Your conversations are recorded and your movements are recorded. GPS tracks where you are and where you were. All of this tracking has and will continue to have an impact on autonomy and privacy. Only recently have governments started to look into the effect that technologies are having on human rights. This area is wide open for future discussion and research. These concerns affect the workplace also. When you worked on the company computer in the company office, it was pretty clear that the company owned your emails. If you are working from home, how much of your personal information does the company have access to? Is it everything that is on your laptop, your tablet or your phone if that device is used for work also? There are many unanswered questions in this new work world.

Our ability to be self-aware, to think about our thinking, is what makes us unique as human beings. As far as we have been able to determine, no other creature has this ability. Science and research may yet prove that this is incorrect. There has been some interesting research done on different species, including whales, which may have an impact in this area. But even if we do find that metacognition is not unique to humans, it is certainly one of our strongest characteristics. It is how we know we are alive. Our ability to live beyond our senses and choose our next thought autonomously is what makes us human. Thinking is how we know what we believe; it is reality translated by us. Our beliefs are thoughts we keep thinking. Facts are beliefs that many people agree upon. Autonomy is your ability to think and then act for yourself.

The latter part of the 20th century made many of us aware that the company could not be trusted or relied upon to keep our best interests at heart. The days of employment guarantees for dedication and commitment gave way to a form of capitalism in the West that supported the philosophy of every person for himself or herself. We saw excessive greed devour economies, massive layoffs, recession and great human suffering. But we also saw humans connect in a way that had never before been possible. Blogs, wikis, social networks and social software allowed the world to open up, communicate and become more aware. Halfway around the globe was not so far away anymore. In fact, it was right next door. Our sense of personal power and our ability to impact others increased.

Your ability to think independently is important now and will become even more important in the future. In your personal life, it will mean making decisions that align with your priorities and then acting on those decisions. In your work life, it will mean buying into company and social goals that are important to you and making your daily tasks meaningful and able to be accomplished. In your relationships, it will mean taking responsibility for how you respond and react, both globally and locally. In your financial life, it will mean questioning, learning and implementing independent strategies that work for you. The new workplace does not offer as many comforts or restrictions as the old one did. It gives you more autonomy and, with that, comes more responsibility for yourself.

Your ability to respond starts with awareness. Once you are aware, you can make choices. If you are unaware, you cannot. Awareness requires you to get in touch with your feelings, actions and thoughts. A lot of research currently says that thoughts contribute to actions and emotions. These are the "big three" that affect character and quality of life. If you are experiencing negative emotions that are causing destruction in your life, or a belief system that makes you feel not good enough, or people who put you down, or behavior patterns that do not support your priorities, you and only you can change this. It is not easy, but it is possible.

Some people think, "I can't do this change stuff, I am too busy." Are you too busy for you? Then do not be surprised if you are not as successful as you might be working and leading virtually. Dividing your day into segments and working with those segments to accomplish your priorities will help you with authentic productivity. It is equally important to clearly define what those results will look like. How will you know you have had a successful day? Will it be by the number of sales calls you made? The number of pages you have written? Items checked off your to-do list? Did you have fun?

Aligning your connections starts with being connected to yourself. When you catch yourself thinking a negative thought or one that is not helping you achieve your priorities, realign it. You can waste a tremendous amount of your day thinking about what is wrong, draining a lot of your productivity. It is almost impossible to be authentically productive when you are stuck in a negative rut. Words have power, so look at the words you are using. Write them down if you think it will be helpful. Remember the internal/external, positive/negative quadrants in Chapter 4? Map it out if you need to. Are you above the line and in the top quadrants? Are you open at the top?

Checking in with you and supporting yourself is essential for success in the virtual environment. It is way too easy to get sidetracked off-task and off-schedule. Whether you are running your own business or working for an organization, you need to check in regularly with your thoughts, feelings and actions. Review your performance over the last 24 hours, then the last week. How are you doing? What have you gotten done? What worked well? What did not work? Don't beat yourself up for every little thing that did not work. Don't forget to praise yourself for those things you have accomplished. Most importantly, be honest with yourself and make adjustments. Go back and review some of those personal project management techniques. Be honest and objective with yourself. See this observation like a movie. Do not judge. If it is not going the way you want it to go, how do you intend to resolve it? Anxiety, fear, exhaustion, depression, stress and a host of other negative patterns will zap your ability to function in the face-to-face world and the virtual world. The difference is, in the virtual world, usually you are the one who has to take the initiative to pull yourself out of it.

It is imperative to support virtual workers just like any other members of your teams or workforce. Virtual workers are and will continue to become an integral part of the business environment. They will come in many sizes and shapes and with a wide variety of skills and human behaviors. These people, whether they work internally or externally, as expert consultants or administrative assistants, will need support to be successful. Fortunately, the technology tools we have available today make the support much easier than ever before. Learning, training, counseling, interviewing and job performance can all be supported using technologies.

Organizations can support virtual workers and teams by providing structure and leadership that can be relied upon and trusted. Clear expectations and objectives that are well-communicated and tracked help the virtual worker understand exactly what is expected. Opportunities to learn and grow are also important to the care and feeding of the virtual worker. Providing training that allows a contribution to the organization's business mission, while aligning with the personal priorities of the individual, benefits both parties. This training serves personal and organizational development in the virtual workplace and can have a significant impact on loyalty and performance.

Collaboration and interdependence in business only come when you have enabled people to be autonomous. People who are dependent are needy and have not bought into the real vision or mission of leadership. If you are a leader in the virtual world, it is your job to make sure everyone knows what is expected. You want to communicate with people early and often, but not be overwhelming. You also need to remember that feedback is a two-way street. Truly collaborative interaction requires feedback going both ways that is open, cooperative and honest. If workers feel they are being criticized, judged or condemned, they will be much less honest and cooperative. If you want collaborative interactions – so important online – you must establish the rules and the techniques to achieve them. Reinforcement and feedback make the pajama worker feel more connected and involved.

The organization needs to support the development of key relationships and provide lots of opportunity for connection and feedback. Feedback was important in the face-to-face environment. It is even more important in the virtual world. You want to know where you stand, if you are doing a good job, and if you are doing what is needed and required to meet the business needs. Leading in the virtual world requires skilled feedback both to the team and individual. Communicating feedback is an art. Positive or negative, it can be a critical component in success. Knowing how to deliver feedback to an individual or team so that it is received the way it was intended requires training. Very few people are experts at providing others with feedback unless they have learned that skill. Feedback should be honest, supportive and timely.

Organizations can also help the virtual worker connect with other people. Human connections and interactions are still the most important aspect of relationships. Knowing closeness with another matters in the face-to-face environment and also in the virtual world. By creating events and exchanges where people can meet and share personal experiences, companies can support individuals becoming closer to other human beings. These kinds of meet-ups do not happen without planning and support. The individual can reach out and connect, but the company can help support those connections. Just like the company picnic and the Christmas party, meeting and having fun, bonding and social exchanges bring people together. When people are emotionally closer, they act more openly and responsibly toward others.

The Pajama Effect is new and different and came upon us very quickly. Somewhere between the early 1990s, when we were just beginning to get connected, and the present day, our expectations changed. We expect different things from ourselves now and we expect different things from others. Our need for connection and gratification on the beach, in the grocery and at the ballgame keeps us attached to devices that run our personal, business and social lives. We expect to be able to get in touch with people anywhere in the world. We expect to communicate from anywhere and with anyone. We expect openness. We expect clarity. We expect understanding. We expect you to be there when we want to connect with you.

The degree and rate of change brought about by technology causes us to question everything. Just a few years ago saying, "I don't know," meant weakness; now it means openness and honestly. No one is an expert for long, no matter what the field. Things just change too quickly. We have come to expect change and to see things in a different light. What was fact yesterday will probably not be true tomorrow. Our attachment to beliefs, ideas and absolutes is giving way to a more fluid frame of mind. In many ways, our expectations are more unlimited. We want to be more, have more and do more, and we expect to be able to achieve this. This boundless environment has made setting our own boundaries even more important. Surprises, insights and discoveries are always just around the corner. Technologies will bring us something new

While we are able to realize a more interdependent planet, it is imperative that each of us is capable and comfortable functioning independently. Our systems and structures may adapt or they may disappear. Many old and established organizations – religious, educational and business – will vanish. Failure is part of creativity and innovation. We live in an environment of innovate-or-perish. The virtual world doesn't have time for pre-judgments and old assumptions. The "shoulds" of yesterday no longer apply to this world. Having an open mind and being willing to do things in new ways is the mode of operation in the pajama workplace. How you thought it was yesterday is not how it is today, and not how it will be tomorrow.

The expectation is that everything is moving faster, which is why it is even more important to slow down. We see, sense and perceive with an urgency that encourages reaction, which is why it is even more important to respond. The respond-abilities support your ability to succeed at whatever you choose. The pajama workplace gives you freedom and responsibility. You are responsible for your flaws, your talents and your strengths. In the pajama workplace, you expect to be more relaxed, less restricted and content. You expect to be in charge of your schedule, your time and productivity. You also expect to be able to succeed.

AFTERTHOUGHTS

These exercises are for you to practice and enjoy. There is
no instant way to transform behaviors. It usually takes
diligence, patience and some effort to change, but it is
possible. It is much less possible if you become
discouraged and negative in your efforts. Celebrate the
little successes and gains. Try not to isolate yourself.
Instead, reach out to others. Humans by nature are
connectors. Remember that you are a pioneer in the virtual
world. The environment and landscape are very different
than anything that has come before in the history of
humans. It is just like the Starship Enterprise landing in a
different galaxy. It takes some adjustments, but over time it
will get to be much easier.

REFERENCES

Altman, A. (2009). The way we'll work: High tech, high touch, high growth. Time Special Report. Retrieved September 21, 2013 from http://content.time.com/time/specials/packages/article/0,28804,1898024_1898023_1898169,00.html

Baggio, B. & Beldarrain, Y. (2011). The blending of work, play & learning online: The pajama effect. Anonymity in Digitally Mediated Communications: Authenticity and Trust in Cyber Education. IGI Publications, Hershey, PA. 155-176.

Baker, G. (2011). Telework – the windfall hidden in plain sight. Retrieved from http://www.us.logicalis.com/pdf/telework-feature-story.pdf

Balanced Score Card.org (2013). Balanced score card basics. Retrieved October 20, 2013 from https://balancedscorecard.org/Resources/AbouttheBalancedScorecard/tabid/55/Default.aspx

Baron, N (2005). Cybertalk at work and at play. Visable Language 39, 1 Education Module 64.

Becker, J. Ballentine, R. Tedford, K. & Lee, A. (2001). Best Practices for managing collaborative technology tools and virtual teams. AMCIS 2001. Proceeding paper 122.

Borowicz, S. (2008). What MBA programs are doing to prepare students to work effectively in virtual teams. Retrieved from http://www.uwex.edu/disted/conference/Resource_library/proceedings/07_5126.pdf

Brown, J. (2012). Learning in hand with mobile technology. University of Wisconsin. Distance Training and Learning Conference 2012. Keynote can be retrieved from http://www.uwex.edu/disted/conference/Resource_library/keynote_resources.cfm

Burns, D. (1999). Feeling good. Avon Books, an imprint of HarpersCollins, New York.

Business Wire (2012). Workplace survey reveals surprises about traditional office life, working from home. Retrieved September, 11, 2012 from http://www.thefreelibrary.com/Workplace+Survey+Reveals+Surprises+About+Traditional+Office+Life...-a0294326001

Capurro, R. and Pingle, C. (2002). Ethical issues of online communication research. Ethics and Information Technology 4: 189-194.

Cash, H. , Rae, C., Steel, A. & Winkler, A. (2012). Internet addiction: A brief summary of research and practice. Current Psychiatry Reviews, 8, 292-298.

Challenger, J. (2002). Blurring the lines between home and work. November – December The Futurist.

Chidambaram, L. & Zigurs, I. (2001). Am I doing what is expected? New member socialization in virtual groups. Our Virtual World: The Transformation of Work, Play and Life via Technology, 40-44.

Cognitive and attentional mechanisms in delay of gratification. Journal of Personality and Social Psychology 21 (2): 204–218.

Covey, S.M.R. (2006). The speed of trust. Free Press, New York.

Covey, S. (1989). The seven habits of highly effective people. Simon and Shuster.

Davis, D. (2008). The Tao of leadership in virtual teams. Retrieved March 12, 2013 from http://teaching.fec.anu.edu.au/mgmt7030/Tao%20Leadership%20and%20Teams.pdf

Driscoll, M., (2004). Psychology of Learning for Instruction. Allyn & Bacon, Boston.

Drucker, P. (2006, 1964). Management for results. Harper Row Publishers, Inc.

Ferris, T. (2009). The 4-Hour Workweek. Crown Publishers, Random House, New York.

Fortier, R. (2009). Telework and rural communicates. Innovisions Canada
http://www.palliseralberta.com/sites/default/files/bob_fortier_-_telework_and_rural_communities.pdf

Fox, M. (2008). Mobile Delivery, Information Any, netconnect.com Fall 2008

Frost and Sullivan Corporation. (2007). World unified communications markets research report. Retrieved May 3, 2007 from http://www.frost.com

Gilbert, J. (2012). Smartphone addiction: Staggering percentage of humans couldn't go one day without their phone, Retrieved September 26, 2013 from http://www.huffingtonpost.com/2012/08/16/smartphone-addiction-time-survey_n_1791790.html

Godin, S. (2009). The Last Days of the Cubicle, Time Magazine, May 25, 2009.

Government eLearning. (2013). Will federal telework programs be challenged? Retrieved October 21, 2013 from http://gov.2elearning.com/gov/news/latest-news/single-news-article/article/will-federal-telework-programs-be-challenged.html

Gregory, I. (2010). Peter Drucker on knowledge worker productivity. Retrieved September 13, 2013 http://www.knowledgeworkerperformance.com/Peter-Drucker-Knowledge-Worker-Productivity.aspx

Gupta, P (2013). Why five days in the office is too many, New York Times, 3/13/2013.

Harrn, A. (2011). What is passive aggressive behavior? Retrieved September 30, 2013 from http://www.counselling-directory.org.uk/counsellor-articles/what-is-passive-aggressive-behaviour

Heffernan, V (2011). Miss G.: A case of internet addiction. New York Times, April 10, 2011.

Hill, A. (2011). Remote control. Retrieved from http://www.telcoa.org.php5-17.dfw1-1.websitetestlink.com/wp-content/uploads/2011/05/Dice-Telework-Report-April-2011.pdf

Innovisions Canada (2011). European telework scene: Stats and facts. Retrieved May 14, 2011 from http://www.ivc.ca/studies/europe/index.htm

Jung, C.G. (1971). Psychological Types, Collected Works, Volume 6, Princeton, N.J.: Princeton University Press. 6, 757.

Kahneman, D. (2011). Thinking fast and slow. Farrar, Straus and Giroux, New York.

King, R. (2013). Yahoo's shocking ban on remote work. Retrieved October 20, 2013 from http://www.linkedin.com/today/post/article/20130225165727-21564708-yahoo-s-shocking-backward-ban-on-remote-work

Kossek. E & Hannum, K. (2011). How flexibility can boost employee productivity. Retrieved September 16, 2013 from http://www.forbes.com/sites/ccl/2011/06/29/flexibility-can-boost-employee-productivity/

Lesonsky, R. (2011). How workshifting is changing the way we work. Retrieved September 13, 2013 from http://smallbiztrends.com/2011/09/workshifting-changing-way-we-work.html

Lister K. & Harnish T. (2010). Workshifting benefits: the bottom line. Telework Research Network: TeleworkResearchNetwork.com

Marshall McLuhan (1964). Understanding Media. Retrieved from http://beforebefore.net/80f/s11/media/mcluhan.pdfMassie, E. (2013). What Do Teleworkers Need as Learners? Retrieved October 20, 2013 from http://clomedia.com/articles/view/what-do-teleworkers-need-as-learners

Meece, M. (2011) Who's the boss, you or your gadget? New York Times, February 6, 2011.

Meyer A. & Meyer D. (2002). CIO Summit. Center for e-business at MIT. Retrieved from http://ebusiness.mit.edu/sponsors/common/2002-AnnualConf/CIOSummitReport.PDF

Mischel, Walter; Ebbe B. Ebbesen, Antonette Raskoff Zeiss (1972). "Cognitive and attentional mechanisms in delay of gratification.". *Journal of Personality and Social Psychology* 21 (2): 204–218.

Murphy, J. (1963). The power of your subconscious mind. Wilder Publications, VA.

Natural Remedies for Total Health (2013). 5 steps for overcoming procrastination. Retrieved October 21,

2013 from http://www.natural-remedies-for-total-health.com/5-steps-for-overcoming-procrastination/

Orenstein, P (2009). The Overextended Family: Is Skype bringing us together or destroying boundaries. New York Times June, 28, 2009.

Pramis, J. (2013). Number of Mobile Phones to exceed world's population by 2014. Retrieved http://www.digitaltrends.com/mobile/mobile-phone-world-population-2014/

Psychology Today (2013). Retrieved September 21, 2013 from http://www.psychologytoday.com/basics/procrastinatio n

Read, D., Loewenstein, G. and Kalyanaraman, S. (1999). Mixing Virtue and Vice: Combining the Immediacy Effect and the Diversification Heuristic Journal of Behavioral Decision Making. December 12: 257-273 (1999).

Roebuck, D. & Britt, A. (2002) Virtual teaming has come to stay – guidelines and strategies for success. Southern Business Review.

Rosen, J. (2010). The End of Forgetting, NY Times, July 25, 2010.

Rosenburg, M. (1986). Conceiving the Self. Krieger Pub Co., 23

Sarkiunaite, I. (2008). Employee communication in organization: IT influence aspect. Retrieved from http://leidykla.vgtu.lt/conferences/europt_2008/files/pdf/sarkiun_410-415.pdf

Sonnentag, S. Mojza, E., Binnewies, C. & Scholl, A. (2008). Being engaged at work and detached at home: A week-level study on work. Work and Stress, 22, 3, 257-276.

Steinfield, C , Ellison, N. & Lampe, C. (2008). Social capital, self-esteem, and use of online social network sites: A longitudinal analysis. Journal of Applied Developmental Psychology 29, 434–445.

Stillman, J. (2011). Scientists prove telecommuting is awesome. Retrieved September 16, 2013 from http://gigaom.com/collaboration/scientists-prove-telecommuting-is-awesome/

Stokes, H. and Wyn, J. (2007). Constructing identities and making careers: young people's perspectives on work and learning. Institute of Lifelong Education, Vol. 26 (5) 495-508.

Suler, J. (2004). The online disinhibition effect, Cyber Psychology and Behavior, 7, 3.

Telework Enhancement Act (2010). Retrieved September 16, 2013 from http://www.gpo.gov/fdsys/pkg/BILLS-111hr1722enr/pdf/BILLS-111hr1722enr.pdf

Thompson, C. (2013) What Marissa Mayer doesn't (and does) get about white-collar work. Retrieved

November 24, 2013 from
http://www.wired.com/opinion/2013/05/fa_thompson

Thurston, B. (2013). Are you a digital addict: Unplug.
Fast Company. July/August 2013 Issue.

The Telework Coalition. (2011). Retrieved May 14,
2011 from http://www.telcoa.org

Turkle, S. (2012). Alone together. Chapter 13 Anxiety,
Basic Books, New York.

Wakeman, C. (2013). Being right is highly overrated.
Retrieved September 26, 2103 from
http://www.forbes.com/sites/cywakeman/2013/04/15/be
ing-right-is-highly-overrated/

Wong, V. (21012). What people really do when they're
working from home. Retrieved April 13, 2011 from
http://www.businessweek.com/articles/2012-06-
25/what-people-really-do-when-theyre-working-from-
home

You Are Not So Smart (2010). Procrastination
Retrieved October 21, 2013 from
http://youarenotsosmart.com/2010/10/27/procrastinatio
n/

Ziglar, Z. (2013). Retrieved October 13, 2013 from
http://www.ziglar.com/search/Goals

Zimmerman, E (2010). Staying professional in virtual
meetings. New York Times, September 26, 2010.

TOUCHPOINTS

LEADING, INSPIRING, & MEASURING PERFORMANCE IN THE VIRTUAL WORLD

1.

Managing the Invisible

"Technology is not technology if it happened before you were born."

--Sir Ken Robinson

In many organizations, leadership is lost. They have little or no idea how to inspire and measure success in the virtual world. They are lost in a paradigm of the past – one that says management has to influence and control to succeed. *Manage* comes from the same root word that is used for *manipulate* or *maneuver*. By definition, it means, "to change something to fit a purpose."

The image of the good soldier willing to sacrifice everything for the cause is still alive in some places. Even in corporate cultures long known for adopting a similar approach, which mentality is beginning to change. Gone are the days of being able to tell if someone is a good worker by how much time that person spends behind a desk. The age of the knowledge worker ushered in a time of "knowing," an era when what was important was in your mind, not on the assembly line. In the last decade, there has been a significant shift in the workplace toward intellectual capital. Along with that has come a reframing of the role of manager as leader.

Good soldiers, you see, were broken. They sacrificed their independence for the cause. Their intellectual spark vanished because they lost something important in the battle of control: they lost the ability to think and act with autonomy. They lost the ability to think for themselves.

In the virtual world, it is essential to be authentically productive. The real reason virtual workers get relocated back to the office is not an issue of collaboration and inspiration, but one of trust. When workers are not in a face-to-face environment, leadership is not sure how to tap into the creativity, innovation and productivity of the workforce. It is not the economy, business cycle, outsourcing or offshoring that is the problem. The difficulty is lack of support and empowerment. Power is the ability to act with autonomy. To create and innovate, you need the freedom to act without judgment.

Innovation in many corporations has become as extinct as Tyrannosaurus Rex. This is a dilemma in a world of constant change, as success depends on adapting to the new. Some companies are waking up to the need to empower workers and inspire them to think independently so they can respond creatively to the relentless change that surrounds them. Others are still operating in a fear-based mentality, afraid of what they cannot see. They are afraid of losing control and afraid of the soldiers deserting. So the Harvard Business Review writes books about innovation and the Economist runs articles on creativity. But what really needs to happen will not be created by edict – it will be inspired by technologies and the freedom inherent in the virtual environment.

Technologies give us the ability to be independent yet connected. You can be at basketball practice in a high school gym in Philadelphia and have a meeting with someone in Japan. If you have a cellphone, tablet or a laptop, and a connection, you can engage in global commerce. Access to world markets is easy. Organizations are starting to understand that managing people who work in this detached but connected environment might require a new approach.

CREATED BY TECHNOLOGIES

Businesses and organizations are using technologies exponentially to communicate and organize "big data" because they can. Their hope is to improve the bottom line either by lowering costs or driving revenue. Technologies provide opportunities to respond to global markets and create them in a way that may be advantageous. Technologies also allow people to interact, engage and share experiences without being physically together. This ability to connect and interact without physical presence is what happens in the virtual environment. These new opportunities and interactions exist because they can.

Changes fueled by an unlimited technology arsenal impact our relationships at work. A global workforce at your fingertips provides both speed and reach, with consultants, microworkers and experts being available to organizations. Compensation practices, the layout of the workplace and job expectations are under scrutiny. Organizations are rethinking what "good" looks like. They are attempting to break down silos, share visions, embrace and not limit vacations, and have casual day every day. The technologies are disruptive; they can change not only where we work, but how.

The virtual workplace is here. Using technologies, more than 50 million people travel less but work just as effectively. They don't have to be in the office and they don't travel for meetings, either. To some extent, these technologies have been liberating. People don't have to be chained to long commutes, sit in traffic or fight the weather. They can work at home in their pajamas if they choose. The new environment is more relaxed, less structured and a freer, more flexible environment than the traditional workplace. Remote access with web-based technologies, collaboration tools and smart devices supports flexible work environments and adaptive schedules. People rely on electronic communication and virtual connectivity to get their jobs done. This reliance on technology has created a double-edged environment: You are both isolated and constantly connected.

That environment also appears to be flatter. People have a direct connection to higher levels of management. Those who were unapproachable in the face-to-face world are a Tweet or email away. There is also a darker side to the virtual environment. It is a world of paradoxes, opposites and contradictions. The virtual leader faces dichotomies that include authority, authenticity, privacy, accountability and identity. The old structures are falling down, but slowly. Like the Coliseum in Rome, symbols from a former era – position, rewards and recognition – still stand in many organizations.

NOT ALL THAT FLAT

We receive personal tweets from rock stars, presidential candidates and football heroes, giving rise to the illusion that, since we adopted social networks, everyone is on the same level and everyone is accessible. Personal devices give us the impression of one-to-one communications. Research on human-to-computer interactions from as far back as the 1960s reinforces that we like to relate to devices in a one-to-one personal way. We relate to the device as if we were talking to another human being – which sometimes we are and sometimes we are not.

Authority is still an issue in most organizations. The hierarchy, chain of command, salary structures and corporate ladders are remnants from a different time. Speed and access are a part of this but the ability to collaborate, or reach and create relationships with other people, is also an influence on organizational change. Collaboration is disrupted by an old paradigm of authority and power. Value in this new world is created through connections with others.

Without the benefits of charisma and immediate authority, managing projects and results becomes less about structure and progressions and more about availability and opportunity. In this new era, many leadership, innovation and change management theories are obsolete because the models are derived from paradigms of the past. Power used to come from hierarchy, position and compensation. The virtual workplace reduces barriers to entry and achievement. Organizational rituals like face-to-face meetings and sitting in the "power positions" at the head of meeting tables or right across from the boss are archaic and outdated in the virtual environment. The traditional ways of relating through control, influence and intimidation just don't work here. The job descriptions of the past don't work, either; that makes organizations in general, and certain people in particular, very nervous. In the virtual environment, there are no corner offices, executive restrooms or preferred parking spaces.

When there are no traditional delineators of power, working relationships tend to take on a new meaning. Authentic productivity and contributions are what count. The traditional chain of command and authority is being challenged. Working in the virtual world tests more than giving up collaboration at the water cooler. It challenges organizations to replace power based on charisma and authority with power based on expertise and contribution. We are changing not only how we manage, but also what we manage. We used to manage people, now we manage results.

Many organizations are reluctant to change. They are content with power networks and visibility that can demand recognition and reward. Traditional notions of executive power and hierarchy are part of Western culture. Most of what is written and researched about virtual teams is based on antiquated team theory from the last century, revisited and updated in a flawed attempt to reflect the virtual environment. Virtual work environments shine a light on the competing values of yesterday and today. It is a challenge for human beings to integrate the new without reference to the context of the old. The virtual environment with all its side-shows – big data, constant connectivity, global reach, boundless everything – creates a very different challenge for leadership. Virtual teams are flatter; they cut across silos and infrastructures. For the last 30 years, organizations have looked to teams to increase performance. Virtual teams are more flexible, creative and fluent. They get a great deal of work done. Technologies enable transition to a virtual workplace, so virtual teams are playing a much larger role in the economics of business.

There is a lot more to the lack of support for virtual workers than just that they are working off-site. Much research conducted in the last decade suggests that organizations are reluctant to give up the hierarchy system. Virtual teams are good at circumventing structure to facilitate speed and availability. Organizational structure can vanish while accomplishing project objectives and goals, but the hierarchy remains because it operates outside of the virtual environment. In many cases it is still alive and well in the C-suite at corporate headquarters. When power and performance are not part of the same structure, this can create problems within the organization. Very little research exists on what happens to power when the organization is horizontal. Up until now, organizations have relied on the past. We have tried to apply centuries-old theories of management and leadership to the virtual environment (Hornett, 2004). Organizations do not want to give up the power structure. This makes it very difficult to manage the invisible.

Having a virtual workforce, however, creates many business benefits for the organization that cannot be ignored. The ability to hire regardless of location, an expanded talent pool, lower real estate costs, a reduction in business and travel expenses, and happier, more productive workers are only a few of these benefits. Workers are happier, have a more flexible lifestyle, and are able to spend more time with their families. It saves everybody money and provides opportunities for people who may otherwise not be able to be part of the workforce. The virtual workplace creates value to the environment as well. It cuts down on gasoline consumption and decreases smog and pollution. But the true value comes from what the virtual worker can contribute, both in knowledge and performance.

Virtual workers struggle with invisibility. They are concerned that what they do is not seen or recognized by the organization's leadership. "Does management know how hard I'm working?" "How do I know what is really going on because no one tells me anything?" They often feel as if they are out of sight, out of mind and out of touch.

Virtual workers also struggle with finding their "off" buttons. A common complaint is, "I feel like I am always on....I am always working." They lack boundaries, both personal and professional, and often feel exploited. Even more, they don't feel as if they are part of the club. Currently, organizations are not very likely to support virtual workers in a way that strengthens them as individuals or as productive performers within the organization.

Working virtually means the worker and the organization need to develop a different set of core skills and competencies. Working in the virtual environment means greater freedom and with greater freedom, comes more responsibility. Workers need the ability to act with autonomy and self-manage. They also need to be able to set and enact priorities, be authentically productive, make responsible choices and align connections (Baggio, 2013). Virtual workers also need the confidence and self-reliance to overcome obstacles as well as the self-discipline and personal project management skills to get work done on time and contribute their expertise. But the organization needs to get involved in this process also. It must encourage autonomous behavior in employees, allowing them to take ownership of their work, their schedule and their performance. Employees need to be empowered and encouraged to succeed. The organization needs to support engagement and productivity through clearly communicated expectations, well-defined performance goals and mutually agreed upon objectives. And then, the most important thing: the organization needs to let employees be free to act with autonomy.

Value is created in the virtual world by offering both flexibility and strong support. Employees must be given the freedom and power to run their own show and balance their work commitments with their personal lives. Management needs to very clear about the business objectives that must be met and the road map to get there. Virtual workers get freedom and flexibility over where and how they live; the organization gets to hire valuable talent wherever that talent resides. Creativity and innovation are only fostered when the mission is transparent and the communications and expectations are clear. At a minimum, expectations need to be more clearly defined, check-ins more frequent, and collaboration more regular. This lowers risk to the individual, stress and fear dissolve, and creativity and innovation flourish. True value is created through encouraging and supporting innovation and creativity. Creativity has a much better chance of thriving in a diverse and global environment. The organization needs to support this talent by developing the skills that give virtual workers the resources to explore a global range of challenges and perspectives.

The biggest challenge to success in the virtual environment is leadership. Leading virtually means leading differently. Leaders in the virtual workplace have to listen between the lines, communicate clearly and intuitively interpret what is being said in the email or virtual meeting. They need to have clear expectations for performance, accountability and measurement, and communicate those. These create the road map for success, so they need to be defined, communicated and reinforced. Leadership also needs to be transparent. Deceitful practices and hidden agendas do not do well in the virtual environment. This is an environment where trust is paramount and lack of trust can sabotage even the best intentions. Trust is difficult to gain and easy to lose. No virtual workplace can succeed without trust in strong leaders.

To manage independent and autonomous individuals, leaders in the virtual workplace need new skills and enhanced capabilities. The old methods do not work. They need advanced communications skills, intuitive listening skills, trust-building and inspirational skills, and, above all, strong project management and accountability. They need to be able to deal with ambiguity and change. They need to reach and connect in a way that supports both the virtual worker and the business objectives. The virtual leader needs to be focused on and deliver results. Value in the virtual workplace is all about delivering the goods. This is achieved by aligning connections. It is the job of virtual leadership to set up enough touchpoints – and the right touchpoints – to get this done.

TOUCHPOINTS

The virtual world is all about connections and connecting. Leaders in the virtual environment need to be effective communicators. They need to build relationships in a world that is fast-paced, remote and where distractions abound. In order to build a relationship, you have to touch someone – not necessarily physically, but certainly emotionally and cognitively. Relationships are built on *touchpoints*, a term used to describe the interface between two things. Companies interface with customers and employees though many different channels: distribution, communication, service, public relations, investor relations or human resources. Virtual leadership is about creating and supporting touchpoints. Touchpoint leadership is a multi-dimensional strategic approach, which focuses on optimizing performance.

Touchpoint leadership creates relationships that support the whole person and meet the business objectives. This is customarily done through roles. People in relationships play roles and this is how they connect. In a sale, someone is the "buyer" and someone is the "seller;" in a friendship, both parties are "friends." In relationships, these roles often come with preconceived meaning. One of the big challenges to leading in the virtual world is developing meaning that works for both sides, yet the traditional management mindset often poses an obstacle to succeeding at that. It's interesting to note that roles are nouns; in the virtual work environment, we focus on verbs. Performance and results are achieved with verbs.

While it is not always easy or automatic to create touchpoints in the virtual work environment, the economics make it an undertaking that can bring positive bottom-line results for both the business and worker. The first step is to get honest and take stock of where you are and where you want to be. Both the individual and the leaders who measure and inspire virtual workers need support. Management's mindset may pose a big barrier to success in the virtual workplace, as fear, loss of control and the "I can't see them, so I can't manage them" mentalities are often denied. What commonly surfaces is a distorted rationale: "We need to be together to bond, collaborate and create." This is just code for, "I don't trust them. If I am not watching them, they are not working and I don't know how to control that or motive these people!"

Touchpoints come in many different sizes and shapes. There are three general categories or types of touchpoints required to lead, inspire and measure workplace performance in the virtual environment: Conceptual, Transactional, and Actual. Conceptual touchpoints include the organizational culture, shared perceptions and views of the organization. Conceptual touchpoints can include many different channels, from branding to social media to any number of internal and external influences. Conceptual touchpoints include the semantics of the organization and the intangible influences that can affect human behaviors. These may be how the organization knows itself, expresses itself and identifies the fundamental things that make it what it is. They can include the little things an individual deals with on a day-to-day basis. There are internal and external conceptual touchpoints, invisible and intangible but still able to affect the individual's performance. Often we attribute these to the organizational culture and the economic climate.

Transactional touchpoints are operational interfaces that impact how work is done. These are the organizational charts, procedure manuals, business processes, operational diagrams, performance requirements or anything else that seeks to capture relationships of importance within the organization. Transactional touchpoints can be the basis for the actual touchpoints but the two should not be confused. Often they are not the same. Touchpoints in the transactional category include the organization's business strategy, political structures, information systems, way of thinking, procedures and frameworks. Companies develop these in many different ways; frequently, these are distinctive to their organizations, people, and markets. These touchpoints are often entrenched in history and seldom examined.

Actual touchpoints are the interfaces that really happen. These are the interactions between leaders and workers, workers and workers, workers and the organizational infrastructure, workers and their performance tasks, and interactions with what they observe or see around them. Vicarious touchpoints are actual touchpoints observed from a distance. Each of these general categories will be broken down into other categories. The labels aren't important. What is critical is that the organization realizes that it touches the virtual worker in many ways: some invisible, some prescribed and some real.

Touchpoints affect the emotional, mental and physical well-being of the virtual worker. These touchpoints can be very supportive and provide reassurance, or very disruptive and contribute to stress and anxiety. There can be too many or not enough touchpoints. They can be restrictive or supportive, imagined or real. The challenge is to establish touchpoints that both support the virtual worker and meet the business objectives. Although flexibility, responsiveness and connections are important, what really matters to business in the virtual workplace is performance results (Rea & Field, 2012).

LISTENING BETWEEN THE LINES

Reaching those results is based on clear communications. Organizations are essentially networks of people joined together through interactions with one another to form relationships through communications of expectations, goals, objectives, deadlines, knowledge, support and efficacy. A wide range of work environments may be considered virtual: global work teams, geographically dispersed project teams, inter-organizational groups, non-traditional workplaces (hotels, home or work centers) and non-traditional roles (microworkers, experts or consultants). Team structures and communication procedures unite or separate in the virtual environment. Organizations and other individuals touch us in many ways. Effective leaders not only know how to navigate within the structures and procedures, they know how to read between the lines (Watson-Manheim & Belanger, 2002).

In the virtual environment, multiplicity is the norm, as workers use a multitude of different technologies and work at a variety of locations. It is also typical to work with a wide variety of colleagues from many different areas. The virtual worker usually works on an assortment of teams and assumes many different roles simultaneously. Each worker may belong to several task forces, work on a project team or several project teams, and belong to a department, division or a work group. The virtual environment is complex and the modes for communication are exploding. Multiple relationships develop and managing these can be challenging. Since communicating via all these different technologies is not the same as being in a face-to-face meeting, the question becomes: What do we need to do to use these technologies effectively and support virtual workers and the organization?

Communication-based work practices are at the heart of performance. These practices can be accomplished through conversations and communicative practices between individuals. How those practices take place in the virtual world depends not only on the people involved but also on the technologies used and how those technologies enable actions.

The importance of relationships and emotional connections in a world geographically distributed is extremely important. Many organizations have a huge challenge with onboarding – acclimating new workers – for this reason. It is important to know who to call when you need something and then how to read the person when they respond. Many people find it difficult to be effective until they know the right people and establish the right relationships. Relationship development is clearly a pathway to success. Collecting information and sharing knowledge affects what teams you get to be on and how you perform. (Watson-Manheim & Belanger, 2002).

Many managers and supervisors in the virtual environment need to learn new communication skills and intuitive listening. The level and effectiveness of this type of listening limits information overload and tries to establish trust and reliance. Creating personal relationships and developing trust when there are limited facial expressions and body language cues requires creating new and different touchpoints. This usually means more communications and touching base more frequently. Regular updates and status reports will help some, but it is the ability to read someone's eyes, face, expressions on video chats and tone of voice in emails that allows you to touch the other person at just the right time and in just the right way.

Like any change, communicating in the virtual environment requires unconventional thinking and a willingness to take a few calculated risks. What we say and what we mean are not always the same. Human beings are complex social animals. They have an inherent desire to know what their territory looks like and how to find their place in it. Often this is done with messages that fly below the radar. Reading these messages takes discipline and a well–tuned willingness to connect with the individual and accomplish objectives. This is a very different mindset than an approach that struggles to maintain control over people, projects and deadlines. Many managers believe that virtual collaboration can actually undermine accountability, creativity and innovation (Rea & Field, 2012). Trust or lack of trust is what happens when we fear we are losing control and when we can't see what is going on. One of the biggest challenges in leading in the virtual world is the change in mindset from managing people's time and activities to managing projects and results.

Let's Look At: Silver, Halpern and Roselle, LLC

Silver, Halpern and Roselle, LLC is a national accounting firm whose main business is in three areas: Accounting, Tax and Audit. Their reputation is excellent and based on great service and trust. Their customers respect them for their advice and stay with them for a long time. This reputation was achieved by state-of-the-art computer systems, analytical databases and a variety of tools the managers and accountants use when consulting with clients. Most of these are custom programs designed for Silver, Halpern and Roselle.

The firm hires expert technical people to develop and maintain the custom applications that support their business. These software applications cover tax laws and coding that is extremely technical and requires attention to detail and a high level of skill. The people who write these custom computer applications must be proficient in both tax law and programming skills. New tax laws are always being applied for the United States and also foreign countries. They must be integrated into the existing systems quickly and flawlessly or the fallout could be very detrimental.

Four programmers work as subcontractors for Silver, Halpern and Roselle. They all live on the U.S. East Coast – in New York, Boston and Philadelphia. The programmers only get together twice a year at the firm's Christmas party and at the summer company picnic. They are connected to each other via email, a synchronous/video-chat platform and telephone. Formal meetings are rare but it is not unusual for informal meetings to occur among the programming staff.

MEET THE STAFF:

George Anderson is a tax lawyer, graduate of the University of Massachusetts and a former hockey player. Married, with three young children and a wife who works full-time in downtown Boston, he is a stay-at-home dad and 35 years old. George has been working for Silver, Halpern and Roselle for eight years and is the oldest and longest standing member of the programming group. He is responsible for all system analytics and design changes. George also functions as the trainer and onboarding specialist. He is the main contact point for the group, the team leader who is responsible for projects being on time and meeting budget. He is busy with soccer games, coaching baseball, dance lessons and basically running the household.

C. J. Creig is a tax accountant, who graduated Boston College with a double major in accounting and computer science. She is 32 years old and has been with the group for two years. She is single, lives on a farm in New Hampshire and loves hunting and fishing. C.J. has a full- time partner and rarely comes into the city.

Margaret Harrison is a tax lawyer and a graduate of the Wharton School of the University of Pennsylvania. She lives in the Chestnut Hill area of Philadelphia and is 29 years old. Currently single, she likes to golf, play tennis and travel. She has been with the team four years and enjoys her autonomy. She works out of her apartment.

Jim Morrelli is a programmer who lives in New York City. His wife is a corporate attorney and they have four children, ages 12, six, four and two. They have a home in town and all the children go to public schools. Jim is interested in his job, but he is also a bass guitarist and plays in a band.

The chief way these people communicate is via email. They send many emails back and forth every day. They can call each other anytime and even the holidays are not off limits.

They meet on Monday morning via video chat and have a rule that when you are online you have the chat stream open. They are all hourly employees except for George, who was made a salary employee last year. They have an agreement that they can work wherever and whenever they want, as long as the work gets done on time. Flexibility and the lifestyles they lead are important to all of them. They enjoy their freedom and none of them plans on ever working in an office full-time again.

Jim is a classic programmer and loves to create code that helps him update the systems more quickly. On a recent project, he created a shortcut that allowed them to get the job done in much less time than usual. A problem arose for C.J., Margaret and Jim when they realized this was cutting into their hourly wages. Rather than tell George, the salaried worker, about the shortcut, they kept it from him out of fear he would tell management and they would make less money. They were able to have more personal time as long as they met the same deadlines and used the shortcut. This all worked well for a while.

Margaret was having lunch one day with a friend who knows several people who work at the firm. During the lunchtime conversation, Margaret leaked that they had an innovative programming shortcut that was giving them more free time for their own interests. Margaret's friend then talked to Art Silver, one of the firm's partners, who became concerned that no one had mentioned this to him. He wondered what the shortcut was and why the billable hours had not changed. He contacted George, who assured him that he knew nothing about it. Rather than making Art feel better, he became more concerned. If George didn't know this, what else didn't he know? Art decided to require everyone to work in the office. Jim and Margaret informed the company they are not about to move. It looks like virtual work is coming to an end at Silver, Halpern and Roselle.

WHAT STEPS WOULD YOU TAKE TO ASSURE THE BEST INTERESTS OF THE FIRM?

1. What is fundamentally wrong with this situation? What steps need to be taken to fix it?

2. How is the virtual nature of the work environment playing into the decisions being made?

3. What impact does technology have here? What other technologies might be used?

4. What steps would you take to change this situation for the better? Is it salvageable? Would you fire anyone?

5. Are there ethical issues here?

6. If you were discussing touchpoints, what would they look like? How might that have affected the situation? How would you change those going forward?

INDEX

About the Author

Bobbe Baggio is a consultant in multicultural and international e-Learning integration for a global and virtually connected workforce. Her area of expertise is the integration of technologies to enhance human performance including adult and workplace learning. She draws upon her experience as a Fortune 100 IT manager, 20 years of consulting experience, and her doctoral studies in instructional design for online learning.

Dr. Baggio is an accomplished author, speaker and educator. Her specific expertise is in how to use technologies to help people learn. She is currently the Director of the Graduate Program in Instructional Technology Management at La Salle University in Philadelphia, PA and speaks regularly to organizations and companies around the globe. Widely recognized as an innovator in the area of instructional technologies, she has published many journal articles, book chapters, a several books.

Her prior experience includes being a Senior Scientist, Director of Distributed IT, Director of Software Development, and a teacher. She has implemented virtual workplace solutions for clients in finance, healthcare, gasses and chemicals, manufacturing, distribution, construction, government and higher education.

Bobbe Baggio

baggio@a-l-t.com

Phone: 610-217-8022

http://advantage–learning.com

CPSIA information can be obtained at www.ICGtesting.com
Printed in the USA
BVOW05s0649170314

347742BV00004B/9/P